HELL IS OVER

HELL IS OVER

VOICES OF THE KURDS AFTER SADDAM

Mike Tucker

THE LYONS PRESS
Guilford, Connecticut
An imprint of the Globe Pequot Press

The Lyons Press is an imprint of The Globe Pequot Press.

10 9 8 7 6 5 4 3 2 1

Printed in the United States of America

ISBN 1-59228-695-X

Library of Congress Cataloging-in-Publication Data is available on file.

To the memory of Mala Mustafa Barzani. And for the Barzani family, whose suffering and survival in Iraq is a history unto itself; for the veteran *peshmerga,* Kurdish guerrilla fighters who fought with him to free the Kurds from their suffering; and to the many Kurdish people who fed me, sheltered me, and inspired me on my travels in liberated Iraq during the summer and autumn of 2003.

And in memory of Senator Robert F. Kennedy, a warrior for justice with the soul of a poet and the heart of a guerrilla fighter.

"But what good is any possession, what good is life itself, if we are not free men? What is life, without freedom? Life without freedom is nothing."

—Ahmad Abdullah Bhadey,
Kurdistan Democratic Party
Military Intelligence officer

"Honor is a real thing, like the air you breathe and water you drink."

—Muhammad Mala Khader,
veteran peshmerga commander

"Truly, we would've fought the bastards with knives and stones, if we'd had to."

—Sanan Ahmed,
KDP Military Intelligence officer

CONTENTS

INTRODUCTION:
Why We Must Listen to the Kurds

I have stared into the wide dark sad eyes of far too many Kurdish children in Iraq who never met their grandfathers and grandmothers because they were murdered by Ba'athists. I have visited many Kurdish mountain villages—roughly, only 500 remain standing of the original 5,000, as a result of Saddam's genocidal terror against the Kurds. I have talked with Kurdish warriors known as *peshmerga*, which means "those who face death." I have listened to survivors of massacres during Saddam's murderous campaign against these proud people. I have discussed the future with Kurds following the liberation of Iraq. Their joy is palpable and contagious—even in these uncertain times of increased terrorism and insurgent attacks. The shackles of their tragic past have been pried free, and still, the Kurds are the unsung, unrecognized heroes of the Iraq War. They deserve better. And we need to listen to what they have to say.

When the American-led Coalition forces seized Baghdad, ending Saddam Hussein's Ba'athist dictatorship, after a twenty-one day campaign that concluded on April 9, 2003, in northern Iraq, a lesser known mission was carried out by Kurdish peshmerga, U.S. Army 10th Group Special Forces, and CIA paramilitary. They assaulted Mosul, home to many key Ba'athists and high-ranking Ba'athist officers in Saddam's army, after a spectacular night riverine raid by the peshmerga, who launched two waves of small black rubber boats across the Tigris River.

Three days later, Mosul fell to the joint 10th Group Special Forces and peshmerga assault force. Unceremoniously, the CIA ordered

Kurdish peshmerga to depart Mosul in the early evening of April 12. Mosul is a city of some 1.7 million divided by the Tigris River, whose eastern banks, comprising 55 percent of the city's population, are Kurdish. U.S. Marines secured the Mosul airfield until relieved in place by the U.S. Army 101st Airborne Division (Air Assault), commanded by Major General David Petraeus, on April 22, 2003.

The removal of Saddam's threat to Kurdish dignity and freedom was richly celebrated by all Kurds, especially by veteran Kurdish peshmerga fighters such as General Babakher Zebari, General Jamil Besefsky, and the legendary Muhammad Mala Khader, men who'd fought gallantly and without pay all their lives against Saddam's Ba'athist dictatorship. These were men who'd buried Kurdish villagers who'd been chemically gassed to death by Saddam's Ba'athist forces in the late 1980s. These were men who'd raided and won against Iraqi soldiers and Ba'athist secret police in deep mountain snows and under scorching highland summer sun from 1961–1991 in an epic guerrilla war. Long before the Bush administration realized the horror of Saddam's dictatorship, Kurdish peshmerga were fighting to end that horror, in the highlands and valleys and back alleys of Iraqi Kurdistan. These were men, as one U.S. Army 10th Group Special Forces commando put it, "who threw down against Saddam's army with nothing but their Kalashnikovs and their balls. And the Kurds are the last men standing, not the Iraqi Army. True guerrilla warriors, who know their history and their people."

Over a year ago, before my travels in Iraqi Kurdistan, I was in Bangkok in April 2003, having earlier been refused embedded journalist status in Iraq with the First Marine Division. I was greatly disappointed on hearing peshmerga had been removed from Mosul, after liberating it. Ba'athists, historically, had deeply feared peshmerga.

Strategically, the American decision to sideline the Kurds denied the Coalition the best intelligence in all Iraq: Kurdish military intelligence. And wars, as Sun Tsu remarked a few thousands years ago, are won in great part due to spies. The better your intelligence, the closer you are to victory in battle. Moreover, I knew enough about Kurdish culture to know that the Kurds would be insulted by America's strange way of saying thank you for fighting to free Iraq from Saddam's tyranny. There is an old saying among warriors: Never betray a comrade. And the Kurds are a warrior culture. I reflected in Bangkok that the Kurds, who were betrayed by American governments twice in my lifetime, in 1975 and 1991, would find no honor in the CIA's actions of April 12, 2003, in Mosul.

Many of the Kurds whose voices are present in this collection have survived decades of guerrilla war, much of it in close-quarter battle, against the Ba'athist regime of Saddam Hussein. The peshmerga fought with uncommon valor, often driving off far superior Iraqi Army forces—superior only in numbers, money, and technology. Statistics mean nothing in guerrilla war.

If we are to win the war in Iraq, we would do well to listen to the voices of the Kurds, who possess *Kurdi zin duah*, which, like the Vietnamese phrase *Dauh Traunh*, means much more than fighting spirit. It means love of homeland, respect and love of family, respect for ancestors and village spirits. We must, ourselves, believe in *Ameriki zin duah*, as Kurdish peshmerga said to me time and again in my travels here—in American fighting spirit and the love of land and culture and freedom that brought us victory against seemingly impossible odds in the American Revolution.

In Iraqi Kurdistan, American and Coalition forces continue to go in harm's way to capture or kill Iraqi insurgents. It was Kurdish peshmerga, of course, who went shoulder-to-shoulder with American fighting men throughout March-April 2003 in Iraqi Kurdistan, as previously noted. Yet Saddam's Ba'athist agents of tyranny, and the terror of al Qaeda and Al Ansar Islam, which were not destroyed during the 101st's time in northern Iraq (April 22, 2003 to January

31, 2004), continue to lash out at Kurds—for the crime of staunchly supporting American and Coalition forces in Iraq. Al Ansar Islam claimed the suicide bombing on February 1, 2004 in Hawlerr, Iraqi Kurdistan. One-hundred ten Kurds died in that bombing. Al Ansar was hammered near the Iranian border by 10th Group Special Forces and Kurdish peshmerga in March-April 2003, but has used bases inside Iran to rebuild and regroup, with the help of al Qaeda, according to General Zebari, former commanding general of 70,000 Kurdistan Democratic Party peshmerga, and Faisal Rostinki Dosky, head of KDP military intelligence.

A longtime friend and comrade of General Zebari, the deeply-respected peshmerga commander Sami Abdul Rahman, was among the 110 Kurds murdered in Hawlerr on February 1, 2004. After the Hawlerr terrorist bombing, imams (Muslim clerics) in Mosul, the Ba'athist stronghold of northern Iraq, preached the following in their Friday sermons throughout February 2004, according to Kurdish military intelligence and Adnan Barwari, a Kurdish activist and translator who was in Mosul during that same time: "Praise the death of the Kurds! The martyrdom operations are joyous! Kill the Kurds, they are dogs and jackals and thieves! When you kill a Kurd, you will receive the same treasure from Allah as when you kill an American soldier! Kill the Kurds, and kill the American soldiers!"

Major General Petraeus liked to use the phrase, in speaking of winning Iraqi hearts and minds in northern Iraq, "money is ammunition." He directed the spending of millions of dollars to that end. In Mosul, since his departure, little of that money appears to have bought any goodwill, much less security. I don't know how many hearts and minds he won in Mosul. But I do know that he did not drive a stake through the heart of Ba'athism in northern Iraq. In terms of crushing and killing the Iraqi insurgency in Mosul, Major General Petraeus fired blanks. His inability to listen to the Kurds, who were fighting and surviving against seemingly impossible odds in Iraq before Major General Petraeus was born, did not aid the Coalition in its continuing struggle to kill Iraqi insurgents.

One such Kurd, who is truly respected by the Coalition, is General Babakher Zebari, now Senior Military and Political Advisor to the Iraqi Defense Minister. I had the privilege of interviewing General Zebari on February 17, 2004 at his headquarters in Dahuk. Silver-haired, spry, vigorous, and keen-eyed, he spoke at great length on the security situation in Iraqi Kurdistan, and all northern Iraq. A few days later, he flew to Baghdad, where he met directly with Ambassador Paul Bremer, Coalition Provisional Authority director, and received his appointment as Senior Military and Political Advisor to the Iraqi Defense Minister.

According to General Zebari, the Ba'athists in Mosul "are nearly as strong, now, as before Petraeus. Petraeus did not listen to us, on this issue. We urged him to strike at the Ba'athists. We told him that disarming peshmerga in Mosul would only open a door for feydayeen Saddam (Iraqi insurgents). He would point his finger at us, and scowl; he thought his degree from Princeton made him God. Well, he was not in line when God was handing out common sense."

And the Ba'athists, who have regrouped under the banner of The Return Party, likely interpreted Major General Petraeus' moves as those born of weakness and insecurity, not strength. Nothing is discounted so much in Arab Beduouin society and culture—and the Ba'athists are Arab Beduouin—as weakness coming from a leader.

Security and counter-insurgency operations, focused on annihilating Ba'athism, were not Major General Petraeus' top priority. I was informed of that by Major General Petraeus himself when I interviewed him in Mosul in August 2003. That was further reinforced by Major Shervington of Strike Brigade, 101st, on Sept. 27, 2003; the major, a tough, witty and eloquent British Army paratrooper who was one of many British warriors in Iraq, wrote out the list of 101st mission priorities, as follows:

- SASO mission: Security and Stability.
- Government infrastructure.
- Building peace: funding schools, health clinics, and hospitals.
- Law and Order/counter-insurgency.

Combat operations were fourth on the list, in order of value. I realized that what Kurdish intelligence had been telling me all along was too true: The insurgents were striking with greater frequency at the 101st in northern Iraq with RPGs, mortars, and small arms because the insurgents saw, daily, that it was not high-priority for the 101st to kill them.

Most unfortunately, Major General Petraeus disarmed in Mosul, in May 2003 the only combat unit in all Iraq with vast experience in guerrilla warfare: the Kurdish peshmerga. After the U.S. disarming of Kurdish peshmerga in Mosul, insurgent attacks rose sharply throughout the summer of 2003. Strategically, the insurgents no doubt saw the removal of the peshmerga from the battlefield in Iraq as a godsend.

I saw no intensity in Major General Petraeus' prosecution of the guerrilla war in Mosul. In fact, Kurdish Military Intelligence had informed me that insurgent fighting spirit in Mosul was the highest it had been, in their estimation, since the insurgents cheered the news that Petraeus had ordered the Kurdish peshmerga in Mosul disarmed, six months previously. Complicating the Kurds' removal from battle by Major General Petraeus was the swift departure from northern Iraq of 10th Group Special Forces, which enjoyed a broad, deep rapport with Kurdish peshmerga and Kurdish political officers of all ranks. 10th Group's exit occurred not long after Major General Petraeus led the 101st north from Baghdad to Mosul on April 22, 2003.

Why was the Coalition's greatest ally to the Kurds removed from combat, in an area of operations that Special Forces not only has vast experience in recently, but one they knew very well from the Persian Gulf War of 1991? I could not get an answer to that question from any American, civilian or military, in Iraq. Perhaps the Bush administration was afraid of the Turkish government's reaction to Kurds ruling in Mosul and Ninevah, and to deepening ties between U.S. Special Forces and the Kurdish peshmerga. The Bush administration likely feared that its NATO ally Turkey, which held sway in Mosul for centuries under the Ottomans and has long oppressed Kurds, would shut down the U.S. Air Force base in Incirlik, Turkey. The fact remains, however, that the Kurds bled with us, unhesitantly. They came though under fire. True warriors, vital to liberating northern Iraq. We remain at war in Iraq. It is a guerrilla war.

An American friend of mine knows the Kurds quite well. His name is Senator Bob Kerrey. He is a tall lean man with silver-gray hair and his grip is strong. He received the Congressional Medal of Honor for his actions in Vietnam as a Navy SEAL lieutenant in 1969. He sat across from me on June 17, 2003, drinking coffee at The Dubliner on Capitol Hill, Washington D.C. Quite generously, he asked many questions about northern Thai hilltribes, and my years in southeast Asia where I lived for over five years.

Near the end of our meeting, he leaned back slightly, squinted and said softly, "Listen to the Kurds. Honor is real. Listen well to them." Days later, he wrote me letters of introduction to Massoud Barzani, President of the Kurdistan Democratic Party, and Jalal Talabani, Prime Minister of the Party of United Kurdistan. A month later I crossed the Harburr River from Turkey into northern Iraq on July 18, 2003. I was overwhelmed by the thanks and praise Kurds heaped on me, simply for being an American in liberated Iraq; the ecstasy of freedom was alive in every wave, every smile, and every warm Kurdish greeting. The Kurds opened their homes and their hearts to me.

On the Iraqi Kurdistan side of the river, I recall handing my passport to a gentleman, who returned it with an open-ended visa enclosed. "You're among friends," he said, and I thanked him before booking a taxi in Zakho, feeling wealthier than King Solomon. I let out a whoop, leaving the building—I was in deep, now, and sky-high. At Sumeir, a small town roughly 25 kilometers south of Zakho, I stopped to change money. Six men inside rose up as one, seeing a small U.S. flag stitched on my vest, and exclaimed, "Thank you, America! Thank you! You are American! Oh, what luck we have to meet a real American!" They settled the fare on my taxi and invited me in for tea.

They were amazed that I'd gotten through; July 3, 2003, had seen the Turks shut the border down completely, incensed at U.S. Army Special Forces seizing Turkish commandos in Kirkuk, convinced they were conspiring to assassinate the Kurdish mayor of Kirkuk. Even on July 18, the day of my crossing, the raid on the Turks continued to dominate Turkish newspapers. I was not entirely surprised; Turkey had never wanted Saddam Hussein to lose power in the first place. The genocide campaigns waged by Saddam against the Kurds meant nothing to the Turks, as they had themselves fought long and bitter counter-insurgency wars against Turkish Kurds since the rise of President Ataturk in 1920. Ataturk banned the Kurdish language, prohibited its teaching in Turkey, and proclaimed that the word Kurd, itself, must not be spoken—that the Kurds are "mountain Turks."

Chief among the Iraqi Kurds' more recent brutal memories is the Turkish Army's love for handing over Kurdish refugees to the Iraqi Army during the horrifying Al Anfal chemical attacks on Iraqi Kurdish villages from the fall of 1987 to the winter of 1988. Chemical Ali, Ali Hassan al-Majid, planned the Al Anfal attacks on orders of Saddam Hussein. Iraqi Kurds have searing recollections of the Turkish Army refusing sanctuary to Kurdish refugees, fleeing Al Anfal, and handing the Kurds to the Iraqi Army. As the veteran peshmerga Salah Ameydi said, "The Iraqis thanked the Turks and killed the Kurds."

Further complicating the issue of Turkish-Kurdish relations, which have great impact on all northern Iraq, is the mindless response of some Turkish and Iraqi Kurds to the long history of Turkish denial of Kurdish human rights—the terrorist response of KADEK, formerly known as the PKK, Kurdish Workers' Party—which has done nothing to aid Kurds. KADEK bombed hospitals, schools, and cafes in Turkey throughout the 1980s and 1990s, murdering Turkish civilians. Today, KADEK is on the same list of terrorist groups as al Qaeda and Al Ansar Islam. KADEK has been formally renounced by both ruling Kurdish parties in Iraqi Kurdistan, the KDP and the PUK. According to Coalition intelligence sources in July 2004, no KADEK terrorists have been killed or captured in northern Iraq since Saddam's fall.

Every Kurd I talked with in northern Iraq, moreover, abhorred the presence of Turkish Army troops. The Turkish soldiers I came across at Ameydi ran toward me and aimed loaded rifles at me when I shot photographs of their tanks and armored personnel carriers (APCs). Holding to an agreement made with Saddam Hussein, the Turkish Army maintains armor and mechanized infantry well inside Iraq, at Ameydi and Bawmarnay, over 25 kilometers inside Iraqi Kurdistan. This, despite the fact that the Saddam-era mandate states Turkish troops cannot go 25 kilometers beyond the Turkish-Iraqi border. The Turkish Army, which refused to help liberate Iraq, has violated its Saddam-era mandate in liberated Iraq on at least two occasions since Saddam's downfall, and sent soldiers deep inside Iraqi Kurdistan. Turkish soldiers and Turkish tanks have no mandate to be on Iraqi soil. The only just and honorable action is to remove the Turkish armor and mechanized infantry from Iraqi Kurdistan.

Given the Kurds deep commitment to America in Iraq and Turkey's inability to honor its December 2002 pledge to America, especially in light of its NATO membership, it is time to ask: On whom can the United States rely in the War on Terror? But given the uneven history between the U.S. and the Iraqi Kurds, the American political and military leadership is incredibly fortunate that the Kurds unhesitantly aided in the liberation of northern Iraq in Spring 2003.

Almost every Kurd I spoke with mentioned, at one time or another, "Kissinger's Betrayal." It is a betrayal that led to the deaths of countless Kurds in March 1975. U.S. Secretary of State Henry Kissinger tap-danced with the Shah of Iran and left Mala Mustafa Barzani and his KDP peshmerga hung out to dry. Kissinger's Betrayal, and the bizarre call to arms against Saddam, and then backing away, of President George H. W. Bush in March 1991 are not forgotten among Iraqi Kurds. The Kurds are looking for U.S. actions on the ground in Iraq which prove that America's honor is real.

To ensure that the Kurds remain an ally in America's War on Terror, where the Middle East is key, America should listen well to the Kurds and not hesitate to accept their aid. The peshmerga possess decades of intelligence—earned in blood—of the remote, mountainous border regions of Iraqi Kurdistan. They know the back alleys in Mosul and bends in the Tigris River like a hawk knows blue sky. The peshmerga know the land, the terrain, the languages, and the cultures, utterly and completely. Their cross-weapons skills, vital to fighting the well-armed and well-financed terrorists of al Qaeda and Al Ansar Islam, are exemplary. And unlike American intelligence officers in Iraq, every Kurdish intelligence officer is perfectly fluent in the languages of Iraq: Kurdish, Arabic, Farsi, and Turkish.

America, finally, should build a major air base in Iraqi Kurdistan. U.S. Air Force Base Incirlik is in Turkey. The Turks, as they proved in the Iraqi War, are unreliable when live rounds go downrange. Unlike Iraqi Kurdistan's neighboring countries, moreover—Turkey, Syria, and Iran—the Kurds are finding no joy on the frequency of radical Islam. The Kurds are, in the words of a U.S. Army colonel in Iraqi Kurdistan, "a goldmine of intelligence in the one part of the world where we desperately need deep, solid human intelligence; we would be fools, and we would pay in blood for such foolishness, not to heed the counsel of the Kurds, and not to take damned good care of them. They know the lay of the land, they know how to fight."

Just as Ba'athism must never regain power in Iraq, for northern Iraq to hold, Iraqi Kurdistan is the key. The Kurds know the region intimately, and most vitally, know how to fight and win at guerrilla warfare. Iraqi Kurdistan borders on Syria, Turkey, and Iran, three borders which al Qaeda and Al Ansar Islam are known to infiltrate across into Iraq. No one knows the ridgelines and mountain passes and desert of all three borders better than the Kurds. For example, Kurdish military intelligence, moreover, captured Hassan Ghul on the Iranian border in mid-January 2004; Ghul is a key al Qaeda terrorist and fundamental to the planning of al Qaeda's horrific September 11, 2001 attacks on America. It was also near the Iranian border that 10th Group Special Forces, along with Kurdish peshmerga, battled Al Ansar terrorists in Iraqi Kurdistan, in March-April 2003.

The Kurds bravely committed all their peshmerga to help America and the Coalition, after the Turkish Parliament refused to honor a December 2002 pledge by the Turkish government to give U.S. forces safe passage across the Turkish-Iraqi border. But the Kurds came through, unflinchingly, providing key intelligence to U.S. and Coalition commanders in northern Iraq and fighting valiantly in Kirkuk, Hawlerr, Mosul, and on the Iranian border.

The Kurdish lifeline, tossed to America as President Bush weathered strong international criticism on the Iraqi War (strongest of all from nations surrounding Iraqi Kurdistan: Turkey, Syria, and Iran), proved crucial. The Kurds, an ancient culture, were great warriors in the war to free Iraq in 2003, as they were hailed ages ago, by

Xenophon in 401 B.C. and Alexander the Great in 331 B.C. In fact, the Kurd's Aezziddian religion, still practiced among a minority of Kurds, is the oldest active religion in the Middle East and its rituals and dances are spectacular, deeply moving, and intensely spiritual. The Aezziddians pray at dawn, noon, and dusk, always facing the sun, their elbows tucked close to their ribs, palms open to the sky. To see the Aezziddian New Year's dance, the same today as it was some 6,000 years ago, is to see magic, melody, and mystery alive and thriving.

And unlike the rest of the Muslim world, the Kurds separate politics from religion. The majority of Kurds, Sunni Muslims, never embraced the idea common to the rest of the Muslim world: that religion and state must be one. Neither have Kurds of other faiths: Aezziddian, Jewish, Shia Muslim, Assyrian Catholic, and Chaldean Catholics. The Kurdish Muslim refusal to heed the political opinions of Muslim clerics flies in the face of the rest of contemporary Islam, particularly Wahabist Islam, the philosophical and religious foundation of Osama bin Laden's terrorist army, al Qaeda.

In July 2004 in liberated Iraq, Kurds speak openly about their love of an Iraq free from Saddam's terror. They never got the chance to speak freely under Saddam's tyranny, and they feared speaking out even during U.N. safe haven years, from 1991 to 2003. I was blessed to listen to the Kurds. The Kurds prevailed over Saddam and now, await the verdict on his war crimes trial. Kurdish integrity, honor, and culture remain intact, whole, uncompromised. May the Kurds live free forever. As the U.S. Army 10th Group Special Forces commando said, "They are the last people standing."

Mike Tucker
Dahuk, Kurdistan
Northern Iraq
August 12, 2004

Book One:

Hard Times, Brave Men

THE LION IN WINTER
Muhammad Mala Khader

Peshmerga fighter, commander, and veteran of the Revolution of 1961
President, Dahuk Branch #1, Kurdish Democratic Party (KDP) Dahuk,
Interviewed: July 23, 2003.

> "The mountain is the only friend of
> the Kurds."

With his white hair and sparkling eyes, large oaken arms and a prizefighter's unsentimental gaze, Muhammad Mala Khader is a legendary
peshmerga. Gesturing with both hands as he leaned forward on his
massive desk, barrel-chested and with eyes that burned right through
me, he spoke with Falstaffian wit and unbounded love of life, rocking
forward in his chair while talking. A living Kurdish treasure, he is well
known for several things: his loyalty to Mala Mustafa Barzani, outstanding combat actions as a peshmerga fighter and commander, and
friend to Massoud Barzani, President of the KDP, former member of
the Iraqi interim ruling council in Baghdad.

The night before I met Muhammad Mala Khader, Kurds had embraced me in the streets of Dahuk. They were jubilant at the deaths
of Saddam Hussein's sons, Uday and Qusay. Even in the morning of
the 23rd, Kurds in Dahuk were still celebrating, beeping their horns as
they drove and shouting, "Death to Uday and Qusay, now, the
Americans will kill Saddam!" Their deaths considerably removed the
threat of any Iraqi return to Ba'athist fascism, and the Kurds rejoiced
in the success of the American raiders in Mosul—Coalition Special

Operations commandos and elite infantrymen of the U.S. Army 101st Airborne (Air Assault) Division.

Between sips of sweet tea, Muhammad was pleased to be interviewed and thanked me for coming "so very far from America." Surrounded by chain-smoking bodyguards while a translator sat to my left, he began to speak swiftly in the poetic rhythms of Kurdish, leaning forward, and raising both arms for emphasis. He'd occasionally pat his Browning HighPower 9mm automatic sidearm in a brown leather shoulder holster under his left arm. "Even now, with white hair and many years behind me, I would still fight, with my 9mm pistol."

■　　■　　■

I am Muhammad Mala Khader! I am original peshmerga, of the ancient warriors! I fought with Mala Mustafa in the Revolution of 1961! I have known brave men in hard times. I have walked with heroes in the streets of Dahuk and the mountains you see. When I was a young warrior, I ran up the mountain like a lion!

And the Iraqi soldiers could not kill me! And I ran down the mountain, swift as a deer! The Iraqi soldiers could not kill me! When I was a young lion, among many lions of peshmerga, I could shoot the enemy's cigarette at 100 meters! Yes, I was a sniper and an excellent shot.

I was born in Hawlerr, in 1934. In Kurdish, we call my city Hawlerr. The Arabs named it Irbil, but it has never been an Arab city. Do we have a Kurdish name for Baghdad, or Basra? Of course not. Since 5,000 B.C., Kurds have been living in Hawlerr. There is an ancient castle, and many United Nations and UNICEF offices.

In 1961, when Mala Mustafa inspired us to end our suffering, I carried primitive small arms, like all peshmerga at that time. From 1961 through 1968, we carried old Lee-Enfields bolt-action rifles. The magazine held five rounds. Also, we carried old German rifles, also bolt action. And a Czech rifle, the Brno, excellent at long-range, accurate and lethal. In that time, we often suffered from a shortage of rounds. Sometimes, they were defective rounds, too. I don't know which is worse, defective ammunition or none at all. A knife is better than a defective round!

But our peshmerga fought wise and bravely. We were fighting against a modern, well-supplied, heavily armed Iraqi Army, and we did damned well in these highlands, in our mountains. We Kurds have a saying, "The mountain is the only friend of the Kurds." And truly the mountains were our refuge and sanctuary.

Then, there was the second era, from 1968 through 1975. In that time, we got RPG-7s! And also, we liberated many weapons from the Iraqis, such as AK-47s. In the third era, from 1976 to 2003, we smuggled in weapons, and also used artillery that we'd captured from the Iraqis.

In 1988, with my men, we were attacked three times with chemical weapons. The Shaqlawa district, near Hawlerr, was the worst for me. I ordered my men to wrap themselves in rough burlap bags. We wrapped rags over our mouths, our eyes, and our noses. The Iraqi planes came, dropping napalm and chemical bombs. There were 300 Kurds in a nearby village. One hundred sixty died that day and one hundred forty survived and they live today but they are terribly handicapped, with disabilities from the chemical weapons. All the world knows of Halapja, yet few people know that there were many Halapjas. Saddam used chemical weapons and napalm on so many villages, Just look at the map and see how many times you see the word "destroyed" under the name of a village in Iraqi Kurdistan. Just look. For so many years, who spoke of our suffering?

In 1969, peshmerga shot down an Iraqi MIG-17 jet. We captured the pilot. So, we sent this pilot to Mala Mustafa. Mala Mustafa was a man of honor; honor is not simply a word in the dictionary, you know. Honor is a real thing, a living thing, like the air you breathe and water you drink. Mala Mustafa told us to never shoot the enemy in the back, and to never shoot a prisoner-of-war. On March 11, 1970, after the cease-fire agreement between the Kurds and Iraqis, the pilot was released, unharmed. He had confessed, under interrogation, that he had indeed bombed twenty-three Kurdish villages.

It is a miracle we survived. Ah, the spirit of Mala Mustafa Barzani sustained us! *Kurdi zin duah!* For us, he was like a great mountain, like the sea in its majesty. You know, when you look at a great mountain or the sea, there is a mystery in it which you cannot truly define. There is greatness at its core, in its depths, in its majesty. And for us, fighting for our dignity and freedom, the spirit of Mala Mustafa Barzani sustained us like nothing else. Let me tell you a story. There was a Kurdish farmer, in the village of Heyzoob, in 1968. He found an Iraqi helicopter pilot, near a helicopter we'd shot down. The pilot wrote out a check for 50,000 dinar and told the farmer to go to Mosul, give them the check, and collect 50,000 dinar. Also, he told the farmer to bring his family to Heyzoob, and he'd get even more reward. But the farmer refused! He told the Iraqi pilot, "I am Kurdish, we are a great people, and you are the enemy of Mala Mustafa! You cannot bribe me!" The farmer tied up the pilot and guided peshmerga to him, who held him as a POW, gave him medical care, and later released him. Mala Mustafa truly inspired our people, and gave Kurds hope for a brighter tomorrow.

For peshmerga, and I believe for all Kurds, Mala Mustafa is greater than the mountain, greater than the sea. And his son, Massoud Barzani, is a fine modern leader for the Kurds, truly he is; he follows the path set by his father, and he is holding us together, with Jalal Talabani and all of the interim ruling council in Baghdad. We walked with Mala Mustafa Barzani in death in these highlands as we walked with him in life. Kurds followed his casket in the huge funeral procession from Iran to his home village of Barzan, here in Iraqi Kurdistan, in 1979. Always with him. Though he'd died, two million Kurds still followed him. He is the George Washington of Kurdistan. It has now been twenty-four years since he died but his spirit is very much alive. Even with our children, just say his name to them and see their reaction! Their eyes will come alive like the stars and they will say his name, cheerfully, and they love him! For we know our history, we Kurds, and we know our heroes. And he is our greatest hero. I was honored to know him, to follow him, to serve him, and I am confident our people will always carry his spirit. Mala Mustafa Barzani will always walk with us, in death as in life. And there is this: Jalal Talabani and Massoud Barzani, the two leaders of our people, now. As you know, this has been a troubled and turbulent relationship. Now, and in the recent past, the relationship is close, good, sound, and open at all levels. We enjoy joint administration, in fact. We fought together, in Operation Iraqi Freedom—the PUK peshmerga and KDP peshmerga fought together in Mosul and throughout Iraqi Kurdistan, to defeat Saddam. There are many people who said this could never happen. That Kurds are our own worst enemies and that we could not come together, to defeat Saddam. But life is full of surprises and some of them are pleasant. I count the defeat of Saddam's dictatorship among such pleasant surprises and I can assure you, our enemies and our critics were somewhat unpleasantly surprised by our victory!

Jalal Talabani actually went to Iran in 1966 and co-operated with Saddam, against Barzani. The recent civil war, from 1994–97, only exacerbated the divisions between Talabani and Barzani. No one can speak of the civil war with pride. But I tell you this: I am very, very optimistic about the Barzani-Talabani relationship, as I am equally optimistic about the relationship between our two parties, at all levels. I strongly hope, deep in my heart, that we never, never fight again. And I hope that the relationship between the KDP and PUK continues on this stable, open, solid road, from now into forever.

And, I make no separation in my hopes and dreams, for myself and for my people! The horizons are open, and we have many hopes for peace and freedom, and the Ba'ath party is gone—I truly hope that our friends in America and Europe stand by us and wish that their support continues. This is a time of many sorrows, and of many, many more joys, many more victories; the Americans just recently unearthed many Kurds murdered by Saddam. This was just three weeks ago in Hatra; yet you saw last night the joy in our eyes, in the streets of Dahuk. And I am sure, in all Iraq, the joy of knowing that Uday and Qusay are dead!

Oh, this is a time of great joy, the joy of knowing our long night of sorrow is over! For this is indeed my great hope, that our great time of joy is now beginning and will carry on, into eternity. You see, most Kurds support democratic federalism, without question. We understand that the Coalition forces delivered us from damnation, the damnation of Saddam. And I believe most people in Iraq support federalism. In my heart, I believe that Kurds deserve an independent state, and when the time is right, we will see that day. Look at Djibouti. So small, yet it is a state. It sits at the United Nations. We have twenty-five million people, in a far larger land, yet we do not sit at the United Nations. One day, we will. But for now, and into the immediate future, federalism is the goal we must achieve. I know that we can, for we are seeing great days of joy, many days of joy, that we fought for. Days we fought for so many years. And we are seeing them with our own eyes. Great days of joy!

QUIET COMMANDING PRESENCE
General Babakher Zebari

Commanding General, KDP Peshmerga, Northern Kurdistan
Interviewed: July 24, 2003

> "We made a vanguard from the blood and
> bones of our dead."

He is a slender man with high cheekbones and a fierce, hard gaze. His hair is silver and his well-trimmed mustache is white. Lines are deeply etched around his eyes. Small in stature yet possessing a quiet, self-contained intensity, General Babakher Zebari was born in 1947 in the village of Birakhaprau in the Akre District. For our interview in his spartan office at the KDP Northern Military Headquarters in Dahuk, he wore a custom-made peshmerga uniform, olive green baggy trousers and a sharply cut fatigue blouse of the same color, and the Kurdish turban was wrapped tightly about his head. A polished cordovan leather Sam Browne belt, of the kind worn by U.S. Army officers up through World War II, crossed his chest.

Behind him, on a wall painted the color of a rising sun in a cloudless sky, there is a picture of his former commander and comrade, Mala Mustafa Barzani, also wearing a Sam Browne belt. Mala Mustafa Barzani is on a white horse, looking out from a mountain down onto a distant valley. Cedar trees stand like a green wall to his right. He holds the wide leather reins of the white horse loosely in his left hand. You can see a pistol holstered and knives jammed in his belt. To Barzani's left in the photo, there is a peshmerga, carrying a long-barreled Czech

Brno rifle in his left hand, an AK-47 slung across his back, and a sidearm in a shoulder holster. That peshmerga is a youthful Babakher Zebari, thirty years before he became Senior Political and Military Advisor to the Iraqi Defense Minister, in July 2004.

"General" in Kurdish is Sarouki. The meaning is closer, actually, to the word "chieftain," in the Irish usage. A Kurdish Chieftain has immense influence among all Kurds. General Babakher Zebari, for instance, is welcomed by Kurdish artists throughout Iraqi Kurdistan; mention his name in the sikehs (bazaars) of Dahuk and Ameydi and Hawlerr and Kurds will nod, musingly, and speak kindly of him. Peshmerga of all ranks warm to his name, and are quick to recollect past raids and reconnaissance General Zebari carried out against the Ba'athist secret police and Saddam's Iraqi Army. He earned that deep respect and affection in over two decades of intense guerrilla warfare, striking at Ba'athists with lightning raids which became his signature style, and for which he is still revered.

■　　■　　■

I have seen the worst of mankind, in Iraq, and I have seen the best, the absolute best that humanity can give. I knew poets who refused to compromise in any way with Saddam, and they suffered for their integrity. And they took their pain with quiet dignity, believing that one day we would all be free from Saddam. Now, that day has come!

We did the job for America in northern Iraq, in all Iraqi Kurdistan. We helped the Americans and the Turks did not. We set up the war front from west to east for the Americans. Especially for the American Air Force, our support was vital to Coalition forces. Moreover, we did not offer them any deal. Our aid was given unconditionally. When Turkey balked, we said to the U.S., "You can build up a base in Iraqi Kurdistan. We are ready to help, unconditionally." We received no ammunition. I commanded 70,000 peshmerga in northern Iraq and we had 27,000 peshmerga throughout all of the Dahuk sector. America took huge advantage of this situation, of course.

About eighty American Special Forces commandos fought with us. The American Special Forces commandos were brilliant, tough, and bold fighters. We lost twelve peshmerga fighters in the fighting, in Dahuk sector. And between sixty and seventy peshmerga were wounded. South of Hawlerr, friendly fire killed twenty-seven peshmerga and wounded forty-five. General Wajee Barzani, son of Massoud Barzani, was seriously wounded by friendly fire. It was tragic but the situation was somewhat chaotic. This is war.

All told, the U.S. Special Forces and peshmerga co-ordination contributed magnificently to the swift liberation of northern Iraq, and all Iraq. Please tell the American people that the Kurds will never forget 10th Group Special Forces, and the 173rd Airborne Brigade. The American commandos liberated us and we were proud to fight with them, to free Iraq from Ba'athism. This is a big, big moment for the peshmerga and for all Kurds, and the Kurdish-American relationship.

Ah, my youth, you know, was a splendid time. I was born in Birakhaprau, just north of the city of Akre. Until 1940, Birakhaprau was still a district capital. But the Iraqi government moved the district capital to Mirgasaur, because the majority of the tribes and villages in Birakhaprau were opposed to Iraqi rule. So, Birakhaprau was a sub-district, when I was born. There was no road to Birakhaprau — the Iraqi government never gave us any services — and my family moved to Nahala. Nahala is the central village for Al Zebari tribe, my tribe. The Iraqis constantly bombed Nahala, shelling it with mortars and artillery. After 1991, and the time of the safe haven, we began to re-build Nahala. We even built a water wheel, to filter our water. I still keep a house in Nahala; it is my mountain retreat. I plan to retire there. It is beautiful. We have many apricot trees, peach trees, nuts, and a great forest.

And the spirit of Mala Mustafa Barzani still walks in my village! What he still means today to the Kurdish people is beyond words. Let me tell you a story. Mala Mustafa was a poet of freedom for Kurds. Many years ago, in the Mahaburat Republic, in Iran, Mala Mustafa Barzani was named Chief of Staff. But, as you may know, the Shah of Iran led a war to destroy Kurds in Iran in the Mahaburat Republic. And the Shah's forces captured Gauzi Mohammad who'd appointed Mala Mustafa as Chief of Staff. The Shah's forces brought Gauzi Mohammad to Tehran. The Shah asked him, "How can you let Barzani become your top general, a country boy, a Kurd?" Gauzi Mohammad replied, "Exactly because he is Kurdish, and he is wise." Later, the Shah asked Gauzi Mohammad if Mala Mustafa would surrender.

Gauzi Mohammad ruled that out, and the Shah became angry with him. The Shah told him that every man has a price, Gauzi Mohammad replied, "Mala Mustafa Barzani is unlike all men in this regard. He will not sell out the Kurds. His integrity is beyond all price. He will never compromise for Kurdish dignity and freedom. Barzani will not give up. He will fight to the last blood of his body." Eventually, of course, Gauzi Mohammad stood before an Iranian judge. The judge tore up the flag of the Mahaburat Republic, in the courtroom, right in front of him.

The Russians had backed the Mahaburat Republic—no one else offered any support—but no longer were aiding Gauzi Mohammad in any way. And the judge spit on the shreds of the flag, and Gauzi Mohammad laughed. This made the judge furious, and he demanded to know why Gauzi Mohammad was laughing. Gauzi Mohammad said, "This flag belongs to Russia. But my flag is in the hearts of my people. And my people will carry it, from mountain to mountain, from village to village, until we are free. And Barzani will live beyond you. Barzani will live forever!"

Yes, Mala Mustafa was a poet of freedom. There is an Arab poet, Saud Hatiz, who is often quoted about him. Mala Mustafa was generous, brave, kind, and tough. He was truly a man rugged as a mountain. By his name, all the world knows the Kurdish people. You see, you can destroy a government, a nation, but not the spirit of the people. The Kurdish people lost so much, so very much to Saddam— 4,500 villages destroyed out of 5,000. On any map you will see the word destroyed with the name of nearly all our villages. And there were many Halapjas, and many mass graves.

But this nation, Kurdistan, made a vanguard from the blood and bones of our dead and we couldn't be destroyed because as long as even one Kurd remains alive, the spirit of all Kurds lives in him, and thrives in him. These are grand, glorious days now for us Kurds and I am glad you are here to share them with us. Thank you for making a brave journey.

LIFE MUST GO ON

Ahmed Hajee Mirkhan Bawarky

Peshmerga, Veteran of the Revolution of 1961
Interviewed: August 12, 2003

> "We survived by fighting—shooting at the
> jets with our ancient rifles."

Ruddy, hatchet-faced, with a jagged scar running across the bridge of
his nose and ending near his thick gray mustache, Ahmed Hajee pres-
ents an easy-going manner, along with a big man's ambling walk. His
bulk dominated the room at the KDP military headquarters in Dahuk.
He has the charisma of the famed New York centerfielder Joe
Dimaggio, lighting up the room with his very presence. Of the original peshmerga who fought with Mala Mustafa, the sixty-nine year old
warrior is deeply respected. An armed peshmerga guard outside the
room came to attention when Hajee passed by—an honor normally
reserved for uniformed peshmerga officers.

Shaking hands warmly all around, Ahmed Hajee exhibited a natural ease with his guests. He had brought bags of fresh grapes and
ripe oranges. Setting the bags down, he reached into a leather vest
pocket for cigarettes and handed them out before sitting back on a
black leather couch.

■ ■ ■

I grew up in the small farming village of Bawarky, an hour and a half
east of Dahuk in mountains near Iran. I watched over some 550 goats

and nearly as many sheep. I had four brothers and three sisters; two sisters and two brothers remain alive. Both sisters are lame, from war wounds, suffered when Iraqi troops attacked Bawarky in Al Anfal, 1988. One is paralyzed, and the other has shrapnel wounds that crippled one of her legs. My paralyzed sister went into a state of physical and mental collapse during Al Anfal after her two sons died in the Iraqi Army's chemical attacks on Bawarky. All of my family's sheep and goats—over 1,000, total—died in the same chemical attacks.

I joined the peshmerga at the end of 1960. By September 11, 1961, I was in the fight. I was fighting the Iraqi Army. My first action against the Iraqis was not far from my home village of Bawarky. Near Ameydi. It was a very difficult battle. We were carrying long rifles, old bolt-action British and German rifles. Fighting against planes. There was much shelling on Ameydi, on the mountaintop city itself. The Iraqis shelled and bombed the mosque; even the mosque was destroyed! Some of my comrades from this action are still alive. We survived by fighting—shooting at the jets with our ancient rifles. We fought the bastards! We were not afraid of the jets. We captured two machine guns from Iraqi policemen. We fired our machine guns at the Iraqi jets. After this battle, we destroyed two Iraqi helicopters. We fired our machine guns at the main blades. We blew the first helicopter in place and cannibalized the second. We used parts from the second helicopter to assemble booby traps, to disable Iraqi Army vehicles.

One of my comrades, Ahmed Josee, from Barzan village [Editor's Note: home village of the Barzani tribe] was an explosives specialist and he was very clever. He would cut the unexploded bomb, for instance, displace its explosive material with water, and remove the explosive material. Then, he'd pack the explosive with TNT, and place two wires in a cigarette pack. The wires ran to an improvised bomb. When an Iraqi soldier would pick up the cigarette pack, the bomb would detonate. Ahmed Josee made many explosive bombs. He was a tough, tough fighter, too. He died fighting in 1975, on the Turkish border, after the collapse of the Kurdish revolution—after Kissinger's Betrayal. Yet we carried on. Our fighting spirit was always high. Still is. It's indomitable!

Yes, our fighting spirit was always the main thing, the main thing! You see, how can you take on and do battle with an enemy who is so vastly superior in weapons, money, and resources? Yet, you can and you will if you are fighting for the dignity and honor and freedom of your people.

Ah, in the first years, it was horrendous. You didn't think of it so much at the time since we were fighting to survive. The Iraqi Army was very strong and some of our own Kurds, unfortunately, the Jash, supported Iraqis. Each family in a village, however, had at least one peshmerga fighter. It was very difficult for the Iraqis to track us—we moved from mountain to mountain, walking ridgelines in the night.

I remember the fighting, very well, in the revolution of 1961. In Zawita, fifteen kilometers from Dahuk [Editor's Note: Zawita is now KDP Special Forces HQ, and was one of the bases for the liberation of Iraq in April 2003] we fought and won a great victory. Oh, it was a great victory! We drove the bastards from Zawita! Then, we met with Mala Mustafa Barzani. I personally handed over the message of victory and our after-action report to Mala Mustafa. You see, we struggled for the sake of Kurdish nationality. The struggle of Mala Mustafa Barzani was our struggle, and every Kurds' struggle. He was our greatest leader.

And his son follows his path. Ah, the outcome of Mala Mustafa Barzani's revolution of 1961 is the victory we are witnessing in, and rejoicing in, today! This moment in history is crucial and will not come again.

You must now know that Kurds are reflecting on and rejoicing in the fighting spirit of Mala Mustafa Barzani! We survived, and prevailed against Saddam, because we kept the spirit of Mala Mustafa alive. But there is one comrade I will never forget. I pray he is remembered. He was an intellectual. His name was Muhammad. He was a great comrade, a fine fighter and a man of deep thoughts. He was witty and a man of sound humor. He was a poet. He was, unlike so many of us, literate. We tried very hard, as years went by, to keep him from the fighting. His ideas were important to us, and we knew that he was a man of great value to us and to our Kurdish revolution. We tried to keep him out of the front lines. Late in the fighting, in 1975, his wife was pregnant. Muhammad insisted he must be in the front lines. He died in combat. His son was born not long after he'd died.

I was shot seven times. And I have one shrapnel wound, from artillery. One bullet smashed my nose, you see [pointing to his nose] but a very excellent peshmerga doctor re-attached my nose and it healed well.

We fought the bastards with anything we could. The British left a lot of small arms here. I carried old British rifle, AK-47, RPG-7, mortars, .57 bazooka, American bazooka, and rounds. I also fired 12.5 AA gun. In Kurdish highlands, our rations were sparse. Rice, dried beef, dried goatmeat, dried mutton, and water. Hot food was a great luxury. There were many times when we fought without food, sometimes for four days at a stretch. We were stronger than the Iraqis, we were tougher, and we believed in our cause. You could see in the faces of the Iraqis that they had no cause, that they fought without spirit. They fought because Saddam held a gun to their back and they knew Saddam would murder their families, their tribes, if they refused to fight.

I will tell you of the most difficult days, in my many years of fighting the Iraqis. There was a twelve-day battle, during Al Anfal—the Battle of Shireen Mountain, a mountain near Barzan village. We were surviving on grapes and tomatoes and water from mountain streams. On the twelfth day, I got a message from Massoud Barzani, telling all Kurds to escape. This was just before the massive chemical attacks of August 1988. I told my men to scatter to the winds and save every Kurdish family they could. With three comrades, I led two large families toward Turkey. All told, we were thirty-two people. Twice, I guided them across a mountain to the Turkish border, on the river, and we were twice denied. The Iraqi Army was right on our heels. Iraqi jets struck at us as we crossed the river; we were strafed and shelled as we crossed. One family's mother was killed in the crossing. A shell made her disappear. Her husband was shocked. He stood in the river like a statue. The Iraqi jets were circling, readying for another run at us. I grabbed and shook him. He was wide-eyed, just shaking, and wouldn't move. I told him that for the sake of his children, he must live. His children still needed their father, I told him. All had now crossed, and my comrades were shouting, so I threw him over my shoulders and carried him to the Turkish shore. The jets strafed us on the Turkish shore but we were very fortunate.

Then, we hid behind boulders until nightfall. My comrades and I gathered grapes and carried water to the families. We ate and moved out. I tried to guide them to a cave on a mountain. The opening to the cave was covered over with foliage. I found a second cave and guided them to it. It was very cold that night. I could see a military camp of the Iraqi Army. They had crossed the border to hunt us down and kill us. At midnight, I watched the Iraqi Army withdraw. The moon was full and high and I could see them, clearly, moving south, toward the river. With a comrade, I searched and got blankets for the women and children, from a Kurdish village. That night, one of the women gave birth to a daughter. The mother needed food and water badly, since she lost much blood in giving birth. She was very weak. Before dawn, we got tomatoes and grapes from surrounding farms. We fed her. She is still alive, today. Perhaps that was the most difficult time of all, when she gave birth. You see, what made it so very difficult was that the woman couldn't make any noise, no noise whatsoever. The Iraqi Army was very, very close. It was within two hundred meters of our cave. We kept her silent, even by force. I was worried that she'd pass out and die. We were all terrified that the Iraqi soldiers would hear her.

The next day, we moved out. Unbeknownst to us, the area had been previously attacked by the Iraqis with chemical weapons. One of my granddaughters, and one of my sons, were so very hungry that they tried eating the wild grass. Then, after several hours, they died clenching their stomachs, with boils on their faces. There was no time to bury their bodies, so we hid them behind stones. The Iraqi jets were still overhead. We returned to the cave and stayed there for seventeen days. We'd move only at night, to forage for grapes and tomatoes. I was the only one who'd go out during the day. I'd use my binoculars and crawl in the woods and high grass, and recon the area. I found a hill with trees overhanging boulders, high on the hill, on the seventeenth day. I returned to the families, and with my comrades, guided them to the hill. We stayed there for thirty-seven days. Everyone was starving, though. Luckily, a group of five peshmerga joined us and together, we decided to make for the Iranian border. At the Turkish-Iranian border, we surrendered ourselves. A Turkish officer fed us rice and grilled beef and gave us hot sweet tea and cool water. It is very strange to talk of this, yet it is true. How strange I thought it was at the time, to feel the friendship of a Turk! Yet he was kind to us, and ordered his men to help us. Perhaps it is because he himself was a Kurd. He spoke Kurdish to us and told us his parents were Kurds.

Life is hard and love is forever. I'm still willing to fight and sacrifice my life for the family of Barzani, who have led us Kurds to the victory we celebrate today.

NEVER AGAIN

General Jemil Mahmoud Suleiyman Besefky

Commander, KDP Peshmerga, Zakho
Interviewed: August 4, 2003

> "Honor is not just a word, it is real as the
> hawk in the sky and the wind on a river."

A heavy-set, broad-shouldered man, General Jemil Besefky is gregarious and jovial. He's big like a retired heavyweight prizefighter, yet he looks the very picture of a Cossack, with gray bushy eyebrows and fierce dark eyes. Gray-haired and deeply tanned, General Jemil, forty-four, carries a Browning 9mm sidearm with black hard plastic checkered handgrips, shifting it off his hip as he sits down on a black leather couch inside an office at KDP Northern Military Headquarters in Dahuk. His bodyguard stands in the doorway, carrying a paratrooper's AK-47. As the commander of 4,000 peshmerga on the Turkish border, at Zakho, he was handpicked by General Babakher Zebari to oversee the reconnaissance, river crossing, and assault, in the Battle of Mosul on April 8, 2003. He spoke frankly of his actions there, along with his years of close-quarter battle and deep reconnaissance as a peshmerga. Our translator was a young Kurdish woman, Bayan Abdullah, who happened to point toward some gold-framed Koran verses on the wall and read out loud this passage in English: "In the name of Allah the Most Gracious, the Most Merciful! Our Lord! We have wronged ourselves. If you forgive us not, and bestow not upon us Your Mercy, we shall certainly be the losers."

■ ■ ■

The peshmerga are not patrolling in Mosul due to Turkish objections. Yet it was the peshmerga who stood by American Special Forces and CIA paramilitary and volunteered our guerrilla fighters to liberate all of northern Iraq, including Mosul. Turkey refused to help America and the Coalition to free Iraq. The CIA controlled the role of the peshmerga, at the beginning of the war. I was surprised, actually, that the Americans gave us the green light, so to speak, to fight in Mosul. I was aware, from the beginning of the war, that the Turks were objecting very strongly to any Kurdish peshmerga participation, and quite aware that the Turks were specifically demanding of the Americans that no Kurdish peshmerga enter Mosul, at all.

But we knew we could make the raid. I had confidence in my men. I'd raided and won against the Ba'athists many times. Just prior to the raid, I'd been on my regular duty, commanding KDP peshmerga in Zakho where I was until April 8th, when I was ordered to report here, to our northern headquarters, in Dahuk. I met with American Special Forces—the 10th Group Special Forces. We made a plan to distribute our forces and advance to Mosul.

I received my orders and led 5,000 peshmerga, first to Badreya, a village roughly halfway between Dahuk and Mosul. We traveled in big open-bed trucks. Near Mosul, I took command of 1,000 men. At 10 P.M. on April 9, I sent forty scouts out on the River Tigris, ten to a boat, to recon the river and report on security. The Americans had previously cached black rubber boats, the boats used small motors. All told, we had fifty boats. My scouts returned and reported the river was wide-open for crossing. I sent them back, to hold the shoreline and guard our approach. Then, my men began to cross. I sent all the boats across in the first wave, 500 men in all. Then, the boats returned and I sent the second final wave across, riding with them. By 2 A.M., all my men were across.

We were the first forces in Mosul. We encountered light resistance, and began surrounding Mosul with our other forces—the 4,000 remaining peshmerga, who were led by American Special Forces. We were doing our best to collect Iraqi POWs, get intelligence to the Americans, and tell the Iraqis that they were not in danger.

By April 10, we had surrounded Mosul, and then we entered Mosul. That day, we got in some brawls with Iraqi Army; we lost fifteen men in the streetfighting, but we secured all our objectives. The next day, I ordered my men to secure N'Zanna, Zumar, Berdeya, Bowushina, and Rabiyya, all villages which are part of the Greater Talafel area, near Mosul. On April 12th, the CIA ordered us out of Mosul, proper. I was very proud of my men. They fought with fire in their eyes. We held all our checkpoints, at the villages mentioned, until we were ordered to withdraw on June 10. I think that when we had seized and held Mosul, perhaps it made it easier for the Americans to secure Baghdad, since seizing Mosul denied Saddam his northern capital. Of course, we were overjoyed to hear the news that the Americans had seized Baghdad on April 9; I will never forget seeing Saddam's statue fall. It was a glorious sight.

We patrolled constantly and seized tanks, shells, artillery and mortars. Unfortunately, many Iraqi soldiers stripped their small arms and hid the broken-down weapons.

The coming of American forces aided both Arabs and Kurds in Iraq, of course. Americans must know that the Kurds are their comrades, and true allies. We put American interests before Kurdish interests. Because, despite our troubles in the past, such as the Kissinger Betrayal, it is due to America that we have been protected, since 1991.

We are writing a new history for the Kurds, now, in my generation. The sacrifices, the suffering past generations endured—all that got us here. I tell you this: If an American is killed, my sadness is the same as if he were peshmerga. It is amazing that we've survived, we

Kurds. For myself, there were two times I thought I'd seen my last sunrise—in the summer and winter of 1982. I cannot say if one was more dangerous than the other. Both times, I was certain of dying. In 1982, on the mountain [Editor's Note: he points to the 4,000-foot mountain behind the KDP Northern HQ] we got boxed in between two Iraqi companies. We were nearly surrounded. It was this time of year, early August. Very hot. We were forty peshmerga, including myself. We had one liter of water. We fought the Iraqis. Running, dodging, climbing the cliffs, trying to hold the highest ground on that mountain. We removed our clips from our AKs and only fired one round at a time. We poured out the water in capfuls and would share one capful, then pass it around. After two days and nights, in that intense heat, the Iraqis withdrew, toward Mosul. Perhaps they'd used all their ammunition, or they'd exhausted all their water and couldn't hang on. But we hung on. This was a key advantage we held over the Iraqis from 1961, on: We were tougher. We were tougher because we believed much more strongly in our people and our land and our cause, and we were harder, much more committed. When you are fighting for your freedom and the dignity of your people, you have nothing to lose. You will fight with all your heart and soul.

The second, equally perilous action in 1982, came in December. We were nine peshmerga, near Berushka village. In the snow and cold of winter. The Iraqi Army surrounded the village. Three comrades were captured alive; myself, and three others, climbed a high tree and evaded the Iraqis, while two other comrades hid in beehouses. Saddam had a policy, strictly enforced, of summary executions of POWs. I never saw those comrades again. I have no doubt the Iraqi Army took them away and shot them.

I now must tell you of my desire to become a peshmerga, the real thing. I looked up to the peshmerga, when I was a young boy, herding goats and shepherding the sheep near Mangkishkee village. I admired Mala Mustafa. He is our George Washington! On February 20, 1980, I joined the KDP peshmerga, after completing my teaching college studies. Sixty of us joined together. In the years since, only three stayed. The rest died or escaped to Iran. Oh, my first eighteen months were hard, always on the run, running and gunning. In the winter, it was most difficult—three of my comrades froze to death near the Turkish border, in late 1981, in the deep snow. They were very weak; we'd run out of rations completely. It was always hard, getting food. Always a hard struggle. At night, we'd get baked bread, and sometimes grilled goatmeat, from villagers. If the villagers knew us, we'd stay. If not, we'd sleep on the mountain. Guerrilla war is very difficult, but we made the best of what we had. I think it is your President Theodore Roosevelt who said, "Do what you can, with what you have, where you are." I always liked that proverb.

I must tell you about a village in Iran. On November 18, 1981, after our comrades died in the snow, we walked into the village of Nuay in Iran. The people in Nuay saved our lives. We were emaciated, exhausted. They gave us hot tea with sugar and salt in it, and hot bread. It was the most delicious bread I have ever eaten. They wrapped us in blankets and kept us by the fires. Nine times I have returned to Nuay to repay their kindness. And I will return to Nuay all my life.

I hope and dream for a bright future for my people. All Kurds believe this is no longer an impossible dream, now that Saddam is gone. We have seen such suffering, unimaginable suffering. Saddam would torture prisoners right in front of their families. His sons would rape women, right in front of their husbands. And kill them.

And I know the enmity of the Turks for the Kurds. In May 1989, I was camp leader of 17,000 Kurdish refugees near Mardin, Turkey. The Turks and the Iraqis devised a plan to kill us, with poisoned bread. For what crime? For the crime of being Kurdish! Our only crime was that we were Kurds. And that is no crime! God created us as a Kurd, as a human being. Even when we'd go to market, the

Turkish soldiers would beat us, going and coming, when we'd go to buy food for the camp. They would always pick out one of us, a good-looking woman, and beat the living hell out of her. We will never, never see that suffering again!

Many, many mass graves have been discovered in Iraq, so many that the Americans cannot investigate them all, at the moment. This is Saddam's legacy, the legacy of death. Oh, the Shias knew this legacy, too, and the Sunni—anyone who believed in freedom for Iraq was an enemy of Saddam. But we Kurds suffered like no one else. The Americans at Hatra [Editor's Note: Hatra is 120 kilometers southwest of Mosul and the site of Kurdish mass graves discovered by U.S. Army 101st Airborne investigators on July 3, 2003.] have determined that nearly all the slaughtered Kurds were women and children. Even a two-month old baby, killed by a bullet to the back of the head. What Hitler wanted to do to the Jews, Saddam wanted to do to us, to exterminate us as a race, as a people, as a culture. Never again will we see the chemical attacks and the mass graves and the trucks driving away in the night, full of Kurds bound to be murdered by Saddam and his Ba'athist evil. Never again! So, my hopes and dreams revolve around securing a future free from the horror we Kurds have seen, with our own eyes, in my generation. To secure a bright future, I think it is necessary to have protection from the United States. Even to be the 51st state of the United States would be a blessing. I hope the American military presence here is eternal, how do you say, in perpetuity. In the past, with the Kissinger Betrayal, there were some real problems between us and America, as you may know. We suffered with the blood and bones of our people, for the Kissinger Betrayal.

We are Kurds and we are surrounded by enemies. The hatred of the Syrians, Turks, Persians, and Arabs for the Kurds will not end simply because Saddam is gone. It is a deep hatred, fueled by their envy of our water and our oil and our unique culture. Kurds are always looking forward; we love our rich past, but we do not dwell on it too much. Above all, I hope and dream and continue to serve as a general of peshmerga so that my children will never witness the horror known to my generation. And the world has long been silent to the suffering of the Kurds. But America was not silent in 2003, no. All praises to Allah. You cannot believe the joy we felt on April 9, raiding Mosul! I dreamed of this day, this action, for so many years. Over two decades as a peshmerga! To liberate northern Iraq from Saddam, ah, truly I am grateful! Know this: Americans will always be remembered as liberators, in our highlands. There is honor in liberation, real honor and joy. Hemingway understood this. Like Homer, he understood honor. Homer knows that honor is real. Read *The Odyssey*. Love is real and honor is real. Honor is not just a word, it is real as the hawk in the sky and the wind on a river. And the liberation of Iraq from the evil of Saddam is a just and honorable action. We will never forget this just and honorable action of the United States.

FIGHTING SPIRIT

Colonel Muhammad Salim Dosky

Veteran Peshmerga and Comander of KDP Peshmerga Special Forces
Interviewed July 30, 2003

> "My deepest dream is that America never
> abandons us again."

Tall and hawk-eyed, the slim Colonel Muhammad Salim Dosky, fifty-nine, enters the room smiling. A translator, who appears half his height, greets him in Kurdish. One of Muhammad's comrades, Ahmad Abdullah, introduces me and we quickly get down to business since Colonel Muhammad has to leave the KDP Northern Military Headquarters, here in Dahuk, to return to his KDP battalion of Peshmerga Special Forces, in Salahadin, later that afternoon. Tea is served and cigarettes passed around. There are other peshmerga—all young men—in the room, armed with AK-47s. I was later told by Ahmad Abdullah that these young peshmerga had never before met Muhammad Salim Dosky, but had dearly wanted to see him. Like Muhammad Mala Khader, he is a legendary guerrilla fighter. Earlier, Ahmad Abdullah Bhadey had told me that Salim Dosky's father was also a legendary peshmerga commander.

■ ■ ■

Yes, my father was a great commander. In my family, I had seven brothers and six sisters. One brother died fighting the Iraqi Army, in

1986. Times are so different now; we are well-supplied, and the rifles are much better. When I was a young peshmerga, in 1963, our old British rifles only held five-round magazines. And always, we were fighting in the mountains. The mountains were our only true friend!

We fought Saddam's soldiers at Khaladizy and shocked them. It was, absolutely, the hardest fighting of my life. Khaladizy is near Sulaymaniyah, the ancient cultural center for us Kurds. We were in the mountains, above Sulaymaniyah.

It was early autumn, 1974. The Iraqis laid heavy siege to us for three days, with continuous shelling by jet planes and artillery. The first twenty-four hours, we had no water. The shelling was intense. Many peshmerga were martyred, on that first day. And the Iraqi Army began to move and attack us. I have little doubt that the Iraqis were confident that the massive bombardment would drive us from the mountain.

And I tell you truly, we lost many comrades in those first three days. But we held! The Iraqis tried to occupy the mountain, but our peshmerga fighters were quite 'excellent sharpshooters, and we laid down accurate and lethal fire as they'd try to move up the mountain. Our snipers still carried the Brno rifle and we made every round count. One well-aimed round can make the difference, when you hold the high ground.

And we held the high ground! Our snipers and our scouts constantly surprised advancing Iraqi elements. We also used our mortars to good effect. I would listen closely to my scouts and move my men in the night, anticipating Iraqi movements. Then we'd hit them in the pre-dawn darkness when they were most vulnerable. Oh, how our fighting spirit sustained us! All the battles I ever fought, all gave me wisdom to hold with our peshmerga at Khaladizy. We fought smart and we fought hard. We stayed there for three months, holding on, to prevent the Iraqi Army from seizing the mountain. Always we raided, in the Battle of Khaladizy. The mountains there are high, and winter came on, and with the winter, snow.

Finally, under orders of Mala Mustafa Barzani, we withdrew. And the Iraqi Army also withdrew; they did not conquer the mountain. Sadly, in the spring of 1975, our Revolution of 1961 collapsed, with Kissinger's Betrayal.

Ah, since 1961, we have struggled! We have faced many difficulties. All of Saddam's oppression operations, all the chemical bombings, all the mass graves. Many people, for example, know of Halapja. No one defended us. More than 5,000 Kurds died at Halapja, from Saddam's chemical attacks. And there were so many Halapjas. So many villages destroyed. So many lives destroyed. The hell of Chemical Ali. And Kurdish people are still suffering from diseases and cancer, from Saddam's chemical attacks. We must capture Saddam and we must kill him!

But now, the U.S. Army has come to protect us. It is a very different time. Now, the destiny of our people is with America. We hope that the Americans see and understand the sacrifices which we Kurds have made with them, to liberate Iraq. And we hope the Americans stay with us, of course.

You know, in the past, many journalists refused to believe us Kurds when we'd tell them about the mass graves and chemical bombings. Now I say to them, come to liberated Iraq, come to liberated Iraqi Kurdistan, and listen to the survivors! We have survived, and prevailed over the evil of Saddam! My deepest dream is that America never abandons us again.

THE HAPPY WARRIOR
Hajee Muhammad Abdullah Ismail

Veteran Peshmerga
Interviewed: August 10, 2003

> "Oh, how sweet life is today! We walk as
> free men."

Hajee Muhammad is a short, wiry, sunken-cheeked man. He walks slowly, with a grave dignity. His deep-set eyes convey a hard-fought wisdom that transcends time and all cultures. He wears the baggy trousers of Kurdish men, a faded canvas and leather vest, and a long-sleeved white shirt. Outside, in the courtyard of the Dahuk Institute of Fine Arts, where this interview took place, stands a white statue of Mala Mustafa Barzani riding a horse. To the left of Barzani's statue is another statue—a peshmerga carrying the Kurdish flag into battle, waving it defiantly, running into battle. Hajee Muhammad, who had carried the Kurdish flag into battle and fought throughout all Iraqi Kurdistan without pay and without hesitation all his life, was the model for the sculptor.

■　■　■

I am sixty and the years were hard. I had four brothers and three sisters. One brother is still alive; he's blind. All my family, otherwise, died in Saddam's chemical attacks in Al Anfal, in August of 1988.

I knew that the peshmerga were responsible for fighting for all Kurds. I knew my duty lay with my people. And I was inspired by

Mala Mustafa Barzani. He led our people on the right path, for dignity and freedom. Long live Mala Mustafa! And I fought until 1987, throughout Kurdistan, for twenty-six years.

I fought at Ameydi, Zebari, Guellyakirkah, Mirayba, Balkerman, near Akre, Guentkay, Sigguerray, Zenovah, throughout the Gara mountains, and Atruz. I fought in many actions, in all those places. I was happy when I was fighting the dictator! I was the happy warrior.

The Iraqis wanted us to bow down. Saddam, especially, wanted us to bow down like dogs. But we are men. And we fought him like men. Now, he is on the run, nothing but a hunted dog, a ghost of a man. And we rule our mountains, not the Ba'athists!

Oh, how sweet life is today! We walk as free men, in our highlands and villages and cities. And we sleep without fear and wake without regret! Yet it is the Ba'athist fascists who watch the night sky and know not if they will see the next sunrise. I say death to fascism, and death to Ba'athists! Ba'athism is a curse from Satan. We must kill Saddam.

My real difficult days were after I was captured by the Iraqi Army in 1987. They captured me near the Iranian border. They took me to the infamous prison camp at Bayharke, near Hawlerr. It was a horrifying place. They would shoot Kurdish POWs, like myself, every day. Always, at least five or ten a day. They would pick us by random. You never knew when your number was up. Some of the Iraqi guards were bribed by Kurds, and these guards would allow food, and blankets, inside. Otherwise, I am certain I would've died from exposure. There were other Kurds there too, not only peshmerga. The widows of Kurdish farmers, the survivors of chemical attacks, and their children—they were with me at Bayharke. We were behind barbed wire. There were guardtowers. It was a place I'd never imagined; a nightmare beyond nightmares.

In 1991, after the safe haven was established in Kurdistan, I returned to my village. My village was gone. There was death everywhere. Dead sheep and goats. Dead chicken. Dead cattle. All the livestock of the village was dead and rotting. And the beautiful stone houses were in ruins. They were at least 1,500 years old [Editor's Note: Tears were running down his face but he did not stop]. Roofs were torn down and walls shelled, mortared, bulldozed. My village was destroyed, like 4,500 other Kurdish villages. And the water was poisoned; Saddam poisoned all the wells of my village.

You asked me of my hopes and dreams. First, I must thank you for coming so many miles, over mountains and sea, to listen to my people. My hopes and dreams are one and the same, for myself and for all Kurds! We must never forget that the bold and daring leadership of Mala Mustafa Barzani paved the way for our deliverance. I hope my people, the Kurds, remember him forever. And I dream that my people never suffer again. That we live with justice and peace and honor, for all time. I hope America does not abandon us, also. My heart soars, every time I see an American soldier. The Americans must know that they made a difference for us, a huge difference, and we are grateful. Their presence is our peace of mind.

COMRADES IN ARMS
Sanan Ahmed and Ahmad Abdullah Bhadey

KDP Military Intelligence officers
Joint Interview: July 31, 2003

"Life without freedom is nothing."

In another life, Sanan Ahmed might have taught history. Or perhaps found work as a hunting guide. He is a swarthy fireplug of a man, copper-skinned and clean in a gray peshmerga baggy uniform. His dear friend, Ahmad Abdullah Bhadey, a cheerful, soft-spoken father of two young sons, might have been a philosophy professor had he not heeded the calling of Massoud Barzani and taken up arms against the dictatorship of Saddam Hussein.

Together, these two men appear high-spirited and jovial, laughing together as tea is served and jokes and stories are told—truly, they are old warriors who have shared hardship and suffering and now, victory over Saddam's Ba'athist dictatorship. When the translator, Nasrrat, enters his office at the Intelligence Branch of the KDP Northern Military Headquarters, Ahmad informs me, "Sanan says, 'You don't look like an American, at all.' He demands to see your passport!"

I fished out my passport from an inner vest pocket, and handed it to the grinning Sanan. He merrily grinned, chuckling, and handed it back to me. Sanan then nodded to Nasrrat, himself a veteran peshmerga and also a Kurdish military intelligence officer.

■   ■   ■

Sanan Ahmed

I was born in Kurumarke village, in 1950. Kurumarke is 25 kilometers east of Dahuk. Not far from Circinck village. I joined the peshmerga in 1964. They refused to let me join, at first. The peshmerga fighters told me, "You must go home. You are still a little boy." I refused! And I started to cry. And I sang song in praise of Mala Mustafa. So, finally, they let me stay. In my village of Kurumarke, eighty young men joined the peshmerga. You know, at that time, we also had the great Joan of Arc of peshmerga. Her name was Margaret. She was brilliant and valiant. A great guerrilla fighter. The Kurds will never forget Margaret. By the way, like you, she was a Christian. From my village, two outstanding peshmerga leaders emerged: Mehmet Ibrahim and Farras Hassin. Farras died four months ago. Mehmet lives.

I was confident we would win freedom for the Kurds. And so we have. I did miss my family. I had three sisters and four brothers. My father and mother missed me, too. They are now dead. One of my brothers was an excellent schoolteacher. He was press-ganged by Saddam's soldiers and forced to the front lines, in the Iran–Iraq War (1980–1988). He died there.

I must tell you, with all my heart and soul, there were two reasons I fought the Iraqis. First, I believed in my people and I loved my people, the Kurds. The second reason is Saddam's evil had to be fought. The Iraqi regime, even before Saddam, was targeting Kurds, even old people and women. And destroying our villages—trying to starve and strangle us. Because of the severe oppression of the Iraqi regime, which increased after 1968 when Saddam took power, I became much more determined—my spirit grew bolder and more determined.

There are things worse than war. I was fighting to conquer those things: oppression, hunger, poverty, evil. My first rifle was a British rifle; it had good balance, and fired eight rounds from a magazine. Bolt-action, semi-automatic. I also carried a Czech Brno, which was a magnificent sniper rifle, and an old German rifle. I learned to fire automatic rifles, water-cooled Fokkhers and the British Bren Gun. The Bren Gun is rugged. I liked it. Truly, we would've fought the bastards with knives and stones, if we'd had to.

There was a battle in 1966 where some of the fighting was hand-to-hand. It is famous among peshmerga. It is the Battle of Zuzek and Hendrin. There were Israeli commandos with peshmerga — I caution you, I was not there. But Farras Hassin was there; I listened to him intently, about ten days after the battle. Before this battle, peshmerga had heard many rumors that the Iraqi Army was drugging their infantry. At the battle, an Iraqi Army division advanced constantly, closing in on us but not over-running our comrades. The most-experienced peshmerga, throughout Kurdistan, rushed to the fighting. I was only sixteen, with but two years fighting behind me, and I was ordered to hold my position, near Circinck. The Israelis helped us well, giving my comrades very good advice; the Iraqis kept coming on, and dying in droves. It was our greatest battlefield victory. My uncle came back from the Battle of Zuzek and Hendrin. Four men from my team, veteran peshmerga, were killed in action at Hendrin. My uncle and Farras sat down with me and told me how our peshmerga fought at Zuzek and Hendrin. Farras was very close to Mala Mustafa; Farras was a very clever peshmerga!

And the gravest situation I faced was on a long-range reconnaissance. My long-range reconnaissance team, in late December, 1987, was ambushed by Iraqi soldiers. Thanks to Allah, we managed to survive and escape. It was a six-man team, including myself. We were on a long patrol in the mountains, in the snow. We had a patrol report to deliver to the KDP in Dahuk of our surveillance of Iraqi Army movements. We were moving very fast, in the deep snow. The ambush occurred near Brawari, not altogether far from Circinck. [Editor's Note: Circinck is 25 kilometers east of Dahuk.]

The Iraqi Army was controlling the surrounding hills. We were coming through a mountain pass late in the night, down a rocky gorge. It was one of our bypass routes, a way we'd used to get around large Iraqi forces, in the past. They ambushed us as we came out of the gorge, into a valley. It was an L-shaped ambush. The Iraqis had at least ten, perhaps fifteen soldiers. They fired AKs and RPGs at us, from our right. The area we were targeted in was very narrow. We were moving two by two. When we were first hit, my point man returned fire with his AK. Our middle two swept left, firing, and our rear two rushed forward, behind them, shooting and moving. We had great experience fighting superior forces, especially in ambushes, and this experience saved our lives. We had planned well for such situations. Also, we were a little lucky. All the Iraqis shot at us, but the bullets went through our trousers! Our culture saved us! You see, all Kurdish men are brought up to wear the baggy trousers. We fired and evaded, running, rolling in the snow. I led my recon team to the small village of Tazeekhah. We took a short rest there and continued on foot, in the night. We delivered our report to the KDP, thanks to Allah. Two of my comrades are still alive, from that night and day on the run. Two died in another ambush. Now, we must find Saddam and kill him. And thanks to American soldiers, I have a very good feeling to live with my family without fear of Saddam's return. Without any real threat, for the first time in my life. And I hope and pray for further, longer, stronger stability. And I agree with my great comrade Ahmad on the matter of America and the Kurds! You see, America can finish its job, can build a great foundation for liberty in all Iraq, by forming a new democratic federal government in Iraq. Put the ministers in place, and open Iraqi embassies around the world. America should stay and finish the job. We Kurds, and I believe many Iraqis, will do everything we can to help America in this effort. I dream that my children live without the suffering and horror, which my generation endured. For Kurds, I can only wish the same, truly. My dreams for my family and my dreams for my people are the same. And I hope my friend and comrade Ahmad Abdullah keeps bringing me grapes and figs from his farm in Bhadey!

■　■　■

Ahmad Abdullah

I was born in the small village of Bhadey, seventeen kilometers north of Dahuk, in 1959. My father was a farmer and carpenter. He was born in 1921 and died in 1989. Like me, he was a revolutionary. As you know, the Kurdish Revolution began in 1961. It was then, in the fall of 1961, when my father was imprisoned, because he was supporting the revolutionary underground. The Iraqi secret police captured him, jailed him in Mosul, and then moved him from one place to another. I was less than two years old when my father was captured. While he was in prison, my uncle took care of my family. I didn't know I had a father until the Iraqis finally released him, in 1968.

The face of my father was like a stranger. My father was brave to stand for Kurdish freedom and dignity. And he was well-known for his deep knowledge of Kurdish history, Middle Eastern history, and geography. Yes, my father was a voracious reader and a self-taught intellectual. He loved to read history, geography, and poetry, especially Kurdish poetry. When I studied Arabic in primary school, my father always helped me to study.

My father helped all my family. I have three brothers and three sisters. My mother was also born in Bhadey, like my father. My mother is still alive. My brothers and sisters are also still alive. And I am married, but I waited until after we had the safe haven, after I had a strong feeling we Kurds would survive. In 1994, at thirty-five, I married my beautiful girl. I had long wanted to marry her, but fighting Saddam, how could we know if we'd survive? We Kurds were alone, for many years. Now, my two sons will live their lives free from Saddam's terror! Oh, these are enchanting times!

In 1969, I lost a year of study, because of the fighting in Bhadey, and near Bhadey. In 1970, I came to Dahuk, and stayed with relatives. I began secondary school in 1970. But the Iraqi Army came in 1974 and occupied Dahuk. The Iraqis were like Nazis. But KDP peshmerga controlled the mountains! There was heavy fighting in 1974, and the Iraqis bombarded with artillery. Iraqi jets and helicopters assaulted Dahuk. As the Iraqis withdrew, however, many Kurds fought them. Oh, how we hated the Nazi Iraqis! We killed them in Grebase, on the western side of Dahuk. Many people in Grebase witnessed the deaths of Iraqi soldiers. Dahuk was much smaller, at that time. And there was no road to Ameydi. The southern foothills, where you see so many houses and shops, now—that was all farmland. After the Battle of Grebase in March 1974, some people of Dahuk joined the revolution. I continued my studies in Ameydi, just over an hour east of Dahuk. It is an ancient city and revered by all Kurds.

Not long after this, there was a terrible bombing at Khaledizy University, near Sulaymaniyah, in 1974. The Iraqi Army killed many students at Khaledizy. So, the KDP leadership, then under Mala Mustafa Barzani, closed schools to keep students alive. Along with many young Kurds, I took my exams in the field of Barmani village, north of Dahuk, to avoid bombardment of our villages and towns.

Throughout 1974 and 1975, my family lived in Stukurky, a village about twenty-two kilometers east of Dahuk, in the mountains. In the summer, we took shelter in the fields, in tents. In the winter, we took shelter in the village. We would hike to Bhadey, about four hours, and harvest our wheat and fruits. But it was a very difficult time. My family, like all Kurdish families, was suffering from napalm bombing, shelling, white phosphorus, and constant artillery bombardment from Saddam's Iraqi Army. We were attacked constantly. There was constant fear. It was a time of unending fear. We could hear voices of the jets from far away. We were burning fires in the winter to stay warm but when we heard the voices of the jets, we'd put the fires out. We built air raid shelters near the village. The shelters had stone walls, sometimes with heavy timbers overhead. We'd camouflage the shelters with grass. Other villages would use caves for air raid shelters

In 1985, not long after I'd finished my university studies, I volunteered for peshmerga. Ah, how I loved the university life. This is an exciting life, the life of the mind. But I knew I must fight for all Kurds. I remember studying, hard and long *The Hero with a Thousand Faces*, by Joseph Campbell. What a wise and wonderful book that is. But what good is any possession, what good is life itself, if we are not free men? What is life, without freedom? Life without freedom is nothing. Life without freedom is mere existence; you are merely counting days.

In truth, our universities under Saddam's rule, like all Iraq, were prisons. Can you cage a bird and know its beauty, truly understand its loveliness? No! The true beauty of a bird is in flight, when it is free to explore and sail on the wind and discover the mountains and river and sky. There, you will see its true beauty. You must free a bird from its cage, to truly know its beauty. I knew that I must help my people win our freedom! *Kurdi zin duah*. I had mused over this for many seasons, in my university days. On April 29, 1985, the Iraqi Army press-ganged me into their forces. I was taken, along with all recent university graduates, to Hilla for six months. Today, the Americans are finding mass graves at Hilla and Hatra, as I'm sure you're aware.

Saddam buried many people, whose only crime is that they were Iraqi and loved freedom, in the mass graves at Hilla. The Iraqi Army ordered me to the frontlines in the Iran–Iraq War, but I took an emergency leave, returned to Dahuk, and joined the peshmerga! Previous to this, I'd long had a good impression of the peshmerga. It was a pleasure to put my recently-gained skills in weaponry to use for the peshmerga.

You know, to train for peshmerga was very hard, especially physically. When anyone joins, it takes several months to train — under constant supervision. We would hike the mountains, night and day. I lost a lot of weight and became fit and strong, like a tiger on the mountains! It was interesting, too, the whole process to become a peshmeraga. First, you contacted the KDP underground. Then, you would have to wait for your security clearance. If you were denied a security clearance, of course you could not become peshmerga. So, after my security clearance was granted, the KDP peshmerga told me that I would receive no salary; that I would often fight without food or water; and that I may die. If I fully agreed to those conditions, without exception, I could sign. I signed.

My initial duties as a peshmerga were demanding, and very grueling. I was happy, I must tell you. I was taking arms against evil. I was fighting the dictator. To fight the dictator is a good and just thing. Like any guerrilla fighter, I held point, carried out reconnaissance, and ambushed the Iraqi Army. This went on for three years, until Al Anfal chemical warfare and genocide operations of the Iraqi Army. The revolution collapsed in the autumn of 1988 and many peshmerga fled to Turkey. I stayed in a camp near Mardin, the same camp in which now-General Jamil Besefsky was the leader of Kurdish refugees. The Turks and the Iraqis poisoned the bread in this camp. Oh, it was a ghastly thing, to try to kill us with poisoned bread.

After the uprising in March 1991, I returned to Dahuk. I saw my village of Bhadey, north of Dahuk. I wept. The old stone houses, which had stood for centuries and centuries, were in ruins. Our fields were poisoned. Carcasses of dead sheep and goats and cattle lay rotting in our fields, the stench was unspeakable. Hell is a real place and its name was Iraqi Kurdistan. Hell is an evil place within the mind. It is what happens when a person turns away from humanity and takes joy in his dark side, in the darkness within him. And then lashes out, in envy and rage and greed and hatefulness, at others, at the world. Hell was also Halapja, and the many unreported Halapjas, like Gizi. The Gizi Massacre. And Bhadey. And Hessee village. I heard the voice of the jets at Hessee village. And I saw the chemical bombs fall from the Iraqi jets. This was on August 25, 1988. I was with peshmerga on a mountain lookout post overlooking Hessee, about 1,000 meters above the village and two kilometers south of the village.

I heard the jets before I saw them. The voice of the jets made an explosion in my ears. And the jets dove over Hessee village, and Akmallee. One jet dove over each village. Each dropped one bomb. The voice of the bombs was not a huge deafening sound. The voice of each bomb was a low rumbling sound. These were chemical bombs Saddam attacked us with, the chemical death. The villagers were crammed together in bomb shelters. They died from the chemicals. I, myself, opened the large, heavy wooden door to one of the shelters. My Kurdish people lay inside, dead. The stench was unbelievable.

Saddam was against all humanity. Now, his past hunts him down, like a shadow he cannot escape. Now, for the first time in my generation, Kurds will begin to know what life is, what joy there is in life. For the first time, we know joy, thanks to America and Britain. And Australia. They lent their commandos to the fight. That was very kind of them. Ah, Australia, land of koala bears and many beaches!

I have never seen an ocean, you know. I would like to walk in the surf on a beach, with my wife and children. Yes, we can speak freely of this great joy, thanks to America and Britain and Australia. These good men came here to liberate Iraq. We consider them as liberators. We believe they will do good for Iraqis and we know the threat of Ba'athist fascism must be removed entirely, to make the region safe. By region, I mean all of the Middle East.

I now must tell you how I met the great Sanan. I met him on the Turkish border, at Mardin camp, in 1988. After 1996, I came to know him well, through our duties with KDP Intelligence. He is a funny man, and a great comrade. And I would be remiss if I did not discuss our terrible years of the KDP–PUK war. We were Kurds fighting Kurds. Both sides were killing peshmerga and forgetting that our real enemy was in Baghdad. All enemies of Kurds—Syrians, Turks, Iranians, and Arab fascists—were happy that we Kurds were so foolish at that time. It was brother killing brother, father killing son, son killing father. A real episode in self-destruction. In November 1996, it ended with negotiations. When the fighting ended, I was on duty in Dahuk. I felt very good, that night. Oh, what joy I felt. We were happy that this fighting would never be repeated again. I held my wife close to me that night and promised her that our children would never see this self-destruction again. My wife told me this must never happen again. She scolded me, and I listened well to her. My wife is a wise woman and she is very right about this. Now, our children will know what life is, what it really is.

Book Two:

From the Ashes

The horror and terror that the Kurds endured under Saddam Hussein's Ba'athist dictatorship came to be known by one word: Halapja. The chemical attacks on Halapja, which killed 5,000 Kurds in the space of one day, March 16, 1988, violated international agreements on the ban of chemical weapons and fully demonstrated, to any who might have previously doubted, the extent to which Saddam Hussein was willing to go to murder all Kurds.

What is far less known, less reported, and even in liberated Iraq not judged as "newsworthy," are the countless murders, tortures, rapes, and other crimes of mass destruction, including chemical attacks, that Saddam Hussein and Chemical Ali (Ali Hassan al-Majid) and the Iraqi Army perpetrated against the Kurdish people.

The greatest weapon of mass destruction in Iraq was Saddam Hussein. His removal from power, and the defeat of his former regime, somewhat removes the threat of Ba'athist revival in Iraq; unfortunately, since May 2003, the Bush administration has allowed key Ba'athist generals to return to power in Mosul and Fallujah, and in government positions throughout Iraq.

The Kurds who survived years of imprisonment as political prisoners—those who witnessed their loved ones raped, tortured, and murdered right in front of their eyes and those who witnessed chemical bombs dropped from Iraqi jets on their villages—are still healing from the barbaric attacks of Saddam Hussein's regime. Should Ba'athism regain power in Iraq, the consequences for the Kurds and all Iraqis who fought to free Iraq would be horrific.

The Kurds remain defiant and unwavering, fully committed to freedom. The Kurds are rising, from the ashes of 200,000 Kurds killed in Al Anfal, to speak freely and for the first time, without fear, of the horror their generation endured, and prevailed over.

In the summer and autumn of 2003, with the Kurds in liberated Iraq, I was fortunate to break bread with these witnesses and listen to their tales of terror and courage.

The Kurds I met were ecstatic, confident, and determined to live in an Iraq where Ba'athist fascism no longer exists.

As I write, underground Ba'athist fascist cells continue to gain strength, according to Coalition special operations sources and KDP military intelligence. Mosul, a stronghold for Ba'athists and the northern city in which Uday and Qusay Hussein thought they'd be well-protected, borders Iraqi Kurdistan.

The small but very well-financed terror network in Iraq has deep roots in Mosul and it would behoove America to listen well to the Kurds, and listen closely to them, if the American government wants to drive a stake through the heart of radical Islamic terrorism in the Middle East. We can win the War on Terror with the Kurds, or we can lose it without them. The consequences of defeat for America in the War on Terror would be devastating; the United States of America would no longer exist. Mosul remains a target of al Qaeda's northern Iraq strategy, for it gives al Qaeda a key base, centrally located in the Near East, with roads and rail lines leading to Syria, Iran, Turkey, Jordan, Saudi Arabia, and of course to central Iraq.

Indeed, Mosul was the destination in late August 2003 of a prime al Qaeda operative, whose base was Hamburg, Germany. The al Qaeda operative, Abdul Kharim, who infiltrated Iraq from

Syria, was arrested by Kurdish police in Dahuk on August 21, 2003 and turned over to KDP intelligence, who then handed him over to the U.S. Army 101st soldiers on August 22 just after seven A.M.

Abdul Kharim was bound and blindfolded, hustled up to the LZ at KDP Northern Military HQ, Dahuk, and flown to 101st Command at Mosul. According to an American military source, Abdul Kharim carried:

> "two huge bags of business suits and clothes, large amounts of cash, a few cell phones, along with personal notebooks, and an obscene amount of expensive cologne. He was well taken care of. Every indication points to him planning to organize attacks on American and Coalition forces, throughout Northern Iraq, including information he's already provided under interrogation. He is a prime catch. He's confessed to being al Qaeda. And the Kurds nailed him."

Given that his capture occurred just after the 101st had received information that two tons of TNT had crossed the Syrian border in mid-August 2003, undetected, the likelihood of Ba'athist fascist terrorists coordinating with al Qaeda inside Iraq is fairly certain.

I needed no further convincing, especially in the aftermath of the car bomb explosion in Hawlerr on September 10, 2003—an attack directed at Americans—which killed forty-two Kurds and wounded many other men, women, and children.

Over the weekend, following that bombing, the Kurdish peshmerga in Dahuk patrolled furiously, scoping the streets from behind 12.7 caliber machine guns mounted in the beds of pickup trucks, peshmerga fighters carrying paratrooper AKs with metal folding stocks scanning in all directions. Large areas of streets were blocked off with cinder blocks, throughout Dahuk.

To defeat the feydayeen, the Ba'athist fascist terrorists, al Qaeda, and Al Ansar Islamic terrorists in Iraq, the Kurds recommend much tougher and thorough actions by American and Coalition forces. The Kurdish consensus is that America should not cage the cobra, it should chop off its head.

"Hunt them down and kill them," said Salah Ameydi, a peshmerga veteran whose son still suffers terribly from chemical attacks near Ameydi in late August 1988. His remarks were echoed by every Kurd I met.

THE WINDS THAT SPEAK

Salah Ameydi

Veteran peshmerga
Interviewed: Ameydi, August 3, 2003

> "Now is a great sunrise after a long night
> of terror and fear."

Salah Ameydi is a wiry man, perhaps 5'10", with intense dark eyes, a drooping black mustache reminiscent of Zapata, and with deep crows feet etched about his eyes. Born in 1960, he has witnessed a lifetime of terror underneath the shadow of fear Saddam Hussein cast on all Kurds. "Do not let them—the Ba'athist fascist terrorists, al Qaeda, and Al Ansar Islamic terrorists—sow fear in Iraq; destroy them, before they cripple and maim our future, as they crippled and maimed our past." Almost a month after this interview, a car bomb explosion in Hawlerr on September 10, 2003—an attack directed at Americans—killed forty-two Kurds and wounded many other men, women, and children.

■　■　■

I have seen many horrors. Ameydi is my hometown. Ameydi was bombed and shelled in 1988, many times. There were chemical attacks on Ameydi, and the surrounding villages in August 1988, such as the attacks on Gizi village. Chemical weapons horribly affected my son. My son is blind, and paralyzed. He was hit with chemical weapons.

I was in the mountains, fighting the Iraqi Army, when my son was hit. He has been blind since 1988, and there is something wrong with his brain. The most difficult thing for me, in all my years as peshmerga, was moving the dead bodies. After the chemical attacks, we were obliged to move the bodies from the fields and towns, and bury them. The horror I have seen. I've seen kids escaping, without knowing the destiny of their parents. Running, terrified, screaming, as the chemical bombs fell. Moving to an unknown destiny. Escaping from the chemical death. Seeing their parents and their relatives fall right before them. Not being able to bury them. Fleeing the chemical death. It was absolute hell.

Now is a great sunrise after a long night of terror and fear. Now, the people in Ameydi are questioning, speaking freely, asking why aren't we a nation? Why don't we have rights—civil rights, human rights, and cultural rights? And why was the world silent in the face of our misery, our suffering, for so many years?

Our Revolution was not in vain! It's important to understand this, if you seek to understand the Kurds and how we are feeling, today. We made the Revolution of 1961 to liberate our people from the suffering imposed on us by many Iraqi regimes. The Americans must stay committed to the Kurds if Iraq is going to stay together. You know, our past with America is difficult; the Kissinger Betrayal of 1975, the ignorance of 1988, and the duplicity and half-measures of 1991 must never be repeated again. Personally, I am hopeful, but not entirely confident, of the Kurdish-American relationship, because of our previous experience. For my people, I say this: the Kurds are waiting for America to keep its word and help prevent the misery and suffering from ever happening in Iraq, again; speed up and intensify all steps to ensure peace, security and stability in Iraq.

The winds speak in our highlands. The story they tell is one of great sorrow and now, great joy. The joy must not die.

GIZI MASSACRE SURVIVORS

Halima Mohsen, Arafat Ramazhan, Yaseen Mustafa Yaseen, and Asia Tahir Kret

Interviewed: August 3, 2003

"Oh, the horror we Kurds have seen!"

The Gizi village massacre is infamous among Kurds. Each survivor I interviewed testified to the rounding-up of Kurdish farmers and their families and the subsequent disappearance of all the males of the village, from age ten and up. The remarks of the survivors of the Gizi Massacre follow, beginning with Halima Mohsen, sixty-five, who, during her tearful recollections, would tug at her long blue dress, her head shaking slowly. She would look up occasionally, drying her tears with a soft white cloth.

■　■　■

Halima Mohsen

Our original village of Gizi is south of here, in the Gara mountains you can see to the south, across the great valley. We grew wheat, tobacco, fruits, and vegetables in our original village, and we had many sheep and goats. Also, chickens. And cows. It was a beautiful village, high in the mountains. On August 25, 1988, the Iraqi Army came. They surrounded our village. They attacked us with the chemicals. We tried to escape but we were all captured. The Iraqi soldiers beat us with their rifles and forced us to walk down the mountain and across the valley. They put us on vehicles, and drove us to Khadesh prison, between Circinck and Ameydi. Then, they drove us to Dahuk prison where there were the Ba'athist party people, and the Iraqi secret police. The Iraqis separated the women from the men. I cried for my son, my husband, and my father. I cried for the men of our village. Oh, all the women screamed and cried. But there was nothing we could do. The Iraqis tortured our men, right in front of our eyes. The Iraqis held guns on us. We could not look away. The Iraqis beat our men with steel cables, with wooden clubs, with leather whips, and with steel chains. Three of our men died, in that first night of torture. After several days, the Iraqi Army drove the women and children to Salahmiyah prison, south of Mosul. We never saw our men again.

We were one week in Salahmiyah. Then, we were driven to Bayharke, near Hawlerr. Only the women and children were transferred to Bayharke. I never, never saw my husband, my son, or my father again. They were taken by the Iraqis and killed. My son was only a teenager. He was only thirteen. He was taken with the men and killed. He was my only son! Why did God let Saddam do this? Oh, my son! [Editor's Note: She was wailing now, then collapsed before two women rushed over to hold her up. She drank a glass of cool water and dried her tears and she glanced south, across the valley, looking for a good while at the Gara mountains far to the south. Her hands were trembling as she gazed at the mountains.]

I still weep for my son. I had three daughters. They married and moved away. And I am alone now. The Iraqis kept me in prison in Bayharke until 1991. I am alone now, I am alone now.

[Editor's Note: I stopped the interview. I told her I was sorry that I'd caused her pain, in remembering the horror Saddam Hussein's Ba'athist army and secret police perpetrated on her and her loved ones and relatives and friends. She reached out a hand, still looking down, still weeping, and I held her hand. She said, "supaz," to me very softly through her tears, the Kurdish for "thank you." A young boy got her some fresh hot sweet tea and she gulped it down. Later, the villagers told me that this was the first time Halima had ever talked with anyone from outside the village about the Gizi Massacre.]

■   ■   ■

Arafat Ramazhan
He was just a boy, eight years old, at the time of the Gizi Massacre. He is twenty-three now and married, with three daughters. He has a reserved, self-contained presence; in the way of Kurds, he is very polite, greeting me in Kurdish and thanking me profusely for being in Kurdistan.

It was misery, misery. All during the end of 1987 and on through 1988, misery. In late August, we heard that the Iraqi Army was coming. Some of us escaped to the Gara mountains. The Iraqis came, and attacked with the chemical death. We ran but they captured us—they had surrounded our village. This was old Gizi. You stand today in new Gizi, which is nothing like our old village. Our old village was idyllic. We were high in the mountains. At night, you could touch the stars. After the massacre, I wondered if I would ever look at the stars again. The Iraqi Army marched us to the main road, and drove us to Khadesh, then on to Dahuk. There were ninety-seven men in the village. The rest were women and children. We stayed several nights in the Dahuk prison. The Ba'athist party officials, and Iraqi secret police, separated the men from the women and children. The men were tortured; we were forced to watch the Iraqis torture our fathers, our grandfathers, our brothers, and our uncles. The Iraqis jabbed the rifle in you, if you tried to turn away, if you tried not to watch. I cried all my tears, in that first night. I never cried again. The Iraqis killed three men by torture, that first night. They were using wood to beat them and steel cables and whips and metal chains. More than five Iraqi soldiers, Ba'athists, and secret police would beat our men at a time. The concrete floor was red with blood. Then, after several days, we were taken on trucks to Salahmiyah, south of Mosul. The Iraqis took our men and killed them and disappeared them.

I never saw my father again. And all of us young boys, all of our sisters and our mothers—we never saw our fathers again. Then, the Iraqis took us to Bayharke. You see, all the children in Gizi, in the new Gizi you are in today, none of them have grandfathers. All of the adults, none of us have fathers. Only one man survived. He is here today. His name is Yaseen Mustafa Yaseen. He is ninety-three years old.

■   ■   ■

Yaseen Mustafa Yaseen

Yaseen Mustafa Yaseen was born in 1910 in the original village of Gizi. He shakes my hand with the grip of a young man and he wears a dark blue woolen cap. His eyes are blue like the sky and he is smiling.

In our original village, deep in the highlands, we feared the Iraqi chemical attacks. Many of our neighbors had already been killed, in the neighboring villages, by the chemical death. On the twenty-fifth of August 1988, the Iraqi Army attacked us with the chemical death. The wind turned, as the small bombs fell; we began to scatter, thinking we might escape. We had nothing to fight them with. They surrounded us, and we surrendered ourselves. The Iraqi soldiers captured us. We walked a great ways, down the mountain and across the wide valley. The Iraqi soldiers drove us on their trucks to Khadesh and Dahuk.

I was among the men who were tortured. We were tortured, one by one. As they beat me with the wooden clubs, I kept saying, "No, no, I am just an old man, let me die in the mountains. [Editor's Note: Yaseen shook his head, casting his eyes down to the ground.

After a few minutes, he glanced up and nodded to me. The translator asked him if he was all right and he told him, "I must go on, yes, I'm all right now. I can finish. If I stop now, the Ba'athists will truly have defeated me. And the Ba'athists did not defeat us! *Kurdi zin duah!* Mala Mustafa Barzani! Peshmerga Brno! Peshmerga Brno!"]

They kept beating me. And I fished out my identification card, and threw it at the feet of an Iraqi Army officer. They kept beating me. Then, the officer ordered his men to stop beating me. And they took me aside. I was the only man in the village, over ten years old, who was not taken and killed. They put me with the women and children, on the trucks for Salahmiyah. We could hear the trucks full of our men, our teenagers, and our sons, pulling away in the night, heading southwest of Mosul. The women screamed, hearing the sound of the trucks disappearing in the night. We knew that sound was the sound of death. After Salahmiyah, they took us to Bayharke. In Bayharke, I re-united with my family—I was on a different truck, from Dahuk to Salahmiyah, and the Iraqis kept me separated from my family, until Bayharke. We survived in Bayharke until 1991, and the establishment of the safe haven. After the creation of the safe haven, the people here in Kurdish highlands have begun to know the meaning of life.

■　■　■

Asia Tahir Kret

Asia Tahir Kret, sixty-one, wears a white headwrap over her head, in the way of some Kurdish Muslim women. Her voice is very soft. Her face is coppered from the sun and her gray eyes are cheerful and warm. Like Halima, this is the first time she has ever spoken to anyone from outside the village about the Gizi Massacre.

I had three daughters and four sons. It is difficult to talk of the Gizi Massacre. You are kind to listen to us. And the world must know the horror Saddam carried out against us Kurds, here in Gizi and all Kurdistan, the world must know! *Balleyyt*. My husband and one of my sons were killed in the Gizi Massacre. My other three sons had escaped from the village. Oh, my beautiful Gizi! [Editor's Note: she was crying now, holding both arms up to the sky, like she was pleading with God.] The last time I saw my husband and son was at Dahuk. The Iraqis tortured my husband and son, right in front of me. The Iraqis held a rifle on me, the Kalashnikov, and I could not look away. They beat my husband and son with steel cables, with whips and metal chains, with wooden clubs! They beat them bloody and senseless. And I could not look away. I could not look away! Oh my husband and son! What crime had they committed? Their only crime was to be Kurds. Our only crime was to be Kurds! *Balleyyt, balleyyt, Kurdi zin duah!*

They took us upstairs in the Dahuk prison and made us watch all night. The Iraqis forced us to watch them beat our men, all night. Three of our men died. As a result of the torture, one of our men had his shirt covered with blood. And the blood began to dry, over his wounds. His shirt could not be removed. I wanted to help him and I called out to him. He said, "No, I will die soon. Pray for my soul. Pray for me. Death to Saddam! We will prevail over the Ba'athists! Death to Saddam!" And they took him outside and killed him. But we did prevail! We prevailed over Saddam! Now, Saddam is on the run like a frightened animal. All he ever is now is all he ever was, a brutal animal! *Kurdi zin duah!*

I still pray for the soul of that man from our village, who defied Saddam, who died for all Kurds. And I still pray for all the men of our village, especially for my husband and son. I still remember the sound of the trucks of our men, pulling away into the desert in the night, southwest of Mosul. The terrifying sound of knowing you will never see your loved ones again. Oh, the horror we Kurds have seen! Capture Saddam and kill him!

ABU GHRAIB PRISON MISERY

Abdul Khader Mustafa Yaseen

Political prisoner
Interviewed: August 3, 2003

> "I saw the blood fall like a river from
> their cells."

A cheerful, slim man, Abdul Khader Mustafa Yaseen, thirty-four, limps slightly as he walks. He was very active in the Kurdish underground as a young man. Here in Ameydi, the morning sun is bright. South of us, across the great valley spreading green and gold from the ancient mountain-top citadel of Ameydi, stand the steep pine-thick ridgelines and rugged gray stone cliffs of the Gara mountains. In his youth, Abdul Khader climbed those mountains. Downhill from the grassy lawn where we sit, gazing south at Kurdish highlands, stand two Turkish tanks and three Turkish armored personnel carriers, manned by Turkish Army soldiers. [Editor's Note: American military and civilian personnel, representing the U.S. government in Iraqi Kurdistan, refused to answer my questions concerning the Turkish Army's Saddam-era mandated presence, as of July 2004, in northern Iraq.]

■　■　■

The Turks are here to spit in our face. They know that all responsible Kurds have renounced the PKK [Editor's Note: Kurdistan Workers' Party]. They know that all ties between the KDP and PKK were

severed, years ago. Think about this: the Turks could not give one soldier, one tank, or one APC to the Americans, to free Iraq from
Saddam. Yet they threatened to invade Iraq, a subtle threat when our
valiant peshmerga rallied to the cause of America and the Coalition.
What bastards the Turks are, to have their tanks here! After all they
did in the refugee camps: beating our women, poisoning our bread,
turning over Kurds to the Iraqi Army to be murdered.

I was working with the KDP underground in 1986, in Dahuk. I
was with the resistance, fighting against Saddam's dictatorship. The
Iraqis discovered my team and captured me. I was seventeen. The
Iraqis changed my ID card, they altered my date of birth to 1968, so
that they could execute me. You see, under Iraqi law, you could not
execute someone if he was under eighteen when he was originally
charged with the crime. I was convicted of crimes against the state
and sentenced to death. The Iraqi secret police blindfolded me,
handcuffed me and drove me to Abu Ghraib prison, near Baghdad.
They tortured me every night. They beat the soles of my feet with
wooden clubs. They put electrical cords on my penis and testicles
and shot the electricity into me. The torture started every night at 1
A.M. It lasted until 3 A.M. The Iraqis did not want to upset their early
morning prayers, so they tortured us in this way. We were in small
rooms. I could hear people screaming.

For my first two years and three months of prison, from April
1986 until July 1988, I was kept in solitary confinement, on death
row. Then, from July 1988 to October 1988, I was kept on death row
in a group cell. There were sixteen other prisoners in the cell, in a
space that was 1½ square meters. There was one squat toilet and one
water tap. It was an incredibly foul place. We were unable to sleep;
ten would stand, while others would crouch, and try to sleep. But
sleep was really impossible. I got my rheumathoid arthritis from this
time, and my heart condition. My doctor told me, years later, "you
were exposed to heavy, hard torture, that is why you had your heart

attack and that is why you continue to have heart disease." I am thirty-four, now, but I've already had one terrible heart attack.

The food in Abu Ghraib was awful: one piece of bread and one bowl of watery soup. Sometimes, rats would get in our soup and we would eat the soup, after the rats had been in it.

The Iraqis were brutal in all ways, but perhaps most brutal in the way they'd select prisoners for execution. The prison guards would hand out bread and soup and then, one of the guards would appear, from out of nowhere, with a plate full of hot grilled rotisserie chicken and fresh steamed rice, and vegetables. Iced orange soda, and cake, and hot sweet tea. And this guard, holding this feast on a tray, would call out the name of one of us. If he called your name, that was your death meal. That is how you knew you'd be hanged that night. Sometimes, the Iraqis would execute en masse. In the case of a mass execution, there would be no death meals. They'd just come in the dead of night and grab prisoners and machine gun them. I remember the Iraqis killing twenty-one of us, in one night. The sound of the machine guns hammering in the night. You could hear the bullets striking concrete, as the Iraqis killed our comrades. There were other incidents like this.

The prison had two levels. There were 1,000 prisoners upstairs. One day, in 1988, a delegation from the Ba'athist fascist leadership of Saddam Hussein entered the second level, drew pistols, and killed more than twenty prisoners. This was in the afternoon. The Iraqis killed the prisoners in their rooms. I was in a cell, downstairs. I saw the blood fall like a river from their cells. The blood ran down and I heard the Iraqi guards laughing.

And I remember when the Iraqi secret police brought the mayor of Baghdad and twenty of his colleagues and they executed him, right in front of us. This was in 1987. You see, they killed us in this way because they enjoyed it! That is the way of a truly evil man; all fascists are this way, they kill first for the sole pleasure of murdering people. Saddam's torture methods were developed in the early 1980s and used extensively, thereafter; his Ba'athist fascist secret police specialized in torturing kids, wives, and family members.

■ ■ ■

Salah Ameydi

[Editor's Note: His good friend Salah Ameydi, who had been sitting quietly, raised a palm toward us, getting our attention. He lit up a smoke and asked, "If I may interject?"]

The Mukhabarat [Iraqi secret police] captured a comrade of mine, from the peshmerga, in 1982. The Iraqis then took him to his village, and captured his wife and eight-month-old baby boy, also. The Iraqis tied up my comrade and his wife. They they stripped my comrade's son and laid him on a table. They put a hot iron on his son until they killed him. Then, they released his wife and four Iraqi soldiers raped her, right in front of his eyes. What torture Saddam used is truly unimaginable. They took my comrade to Abu Ghraib also. After a few years, he was released and found his wife. She is a very tough woman and somehow, she had kept her body and soul together. They escaped together across the Turkish border and made their way to some of our comrades in Sweden, where they still live today.

■ ■ ■

Kurdistan Political Prisoners Union
Opening Ceremonies of the Ameydi Branch
Ameydi, Iraqi Kurdistan, Northern Iraq
August 19, 2003 10:15 A.M.

On the second floor of a concrete-walled, spartanly furnished building, Kurdish men and women gathered in a dimly-lit hall to celebrate the defeat of Saddam Hussein's dictatorship and the opening of a new branch of the Kurdistan Political Prisoners Union.

Salah Ameydi and Abdul Khader greeted me and Fawsi Mohammad, a friend of mine from Dahuk who was also a former political prisoner at Abu Ghraib, shook their hands and joked with them as he offered cigarettes.

Amidst a flurry of back-slapping and warm greetings, cigarette smoke, and quickly-gulped hot sweet tea, a slim man who was perhaps 5'7" and wearing a black two-button suit stepped up to a platform at the front of the hall and greeted everyone in Kurdish.

Fawsi motioned for us to take seats up front and I found a seat behind two Americans from Special Operations, Chris and Tony—their full names and ranks cannot be given, to ensure operational security—who were attached to a U.S. Army Civil Affairs unit operating in Iraqi Kurdistan.

Before the gentleman in the black suit spoke, Chris spoke briefly about his work with the Kurds: "We have received, no question, the most excellent reception from Kurds throughout Iraqi Kurdistan. They have been generous and patient and brave. And the kindness and hospitality we've received can only be defined by one word: phenomenal."

Chris and Tony asked me about my work in Iraqi Kurdistan, briefly, before the man in black spoke softly into the microphone; quiet came quickly over the crowd and there was a silent wave of respect directed immediately toward the gentleman on the platform.

His name was Amin Ismail and he was famed in Kurdistan for his resistance to the Iraqi secret police. For his refusal to bow down to Saddam Hussein's Ba'athist fascist dictatorship, Amin served thirteen years in abominable conditions in Dahuk, Kirkuk, and Abu Ghraib.

He called for a moment of silence for all Kurdish political prisoners who were murdered by Saddam Hussein's Ba'athist secret police, and by the Iraqi Army. And for all Kurds who were murdered by the Iraqi Army, Ba'athist secret police, and other Iraqi security forces during Saddam Hussein's thirty-five year reign of terror.

We all bowed heads and prayers were whispered and Amin said softly that the suffering of all Kurdish political prisoners, the living and the dead, will never be forgotten.

He ended with a salute to Mala Mustafa Barzani, and declared, raising a fist and smiling, "The spirit of Mala Mustafa, of freedom and dignity, endures forever! Long live Mala Mustafa!"

The hall erupted with cheers and bravos. White-haired peshmerga veterans behind me, in custom-tailored olive green baggy trousers and fatigue blouses over collared shirts, wearing white and black checked turbans, shook my hand and we exchanged greetings in Kurdish before again taking seats.

From the platform, Amin decreed the new branch open, and asked for Fawsi Mohammad to give the opening remarks.

Fawsi's remarks were short and to the point: "Saddam beat us, he tortured us, but we survived. In the end, *we* defeated him! Now, we celebrate our freedom and honor the sacrifice of our comrades, our men and women and children, whose suffering we will never forget. Long may our brothers and sisters in Ameydi rejoice in freedom and dignity! Long live Mala Mustafa Barzani!"

Again, the hall erupted with cheers and Fawsi, returning to his seat, winked and asked, "Do you think they agree with me, brother?" I nodded, grinning, and he laughed as he turned and shook hands with the peshmerga veterans behind us.

Amin quieted the crowd and began reading a poem by the famed Kurdish poet Bader Khan Sindi, a poem "Kurdish political prisoners would whisper to one another in the darkness of Abu Ghraib," Fawsi said as Amin began to read.

Amin's voice was soft-toned, understated, and everyone in the Hall was quiet and attentive as he recited the poem in Kurdish. I remember thinking of Amin's own torture, as he read the poem. I'd interviewed him the day before, in Dahuk, thanks to Fawsi Mohammad and Lieutenant Colonel Randal Campbell, of the U.S. Army 101st Airborne Division (Air Assault). In Dahuk on the eighteenth, a young lady with a white headwrap, in a long purple dress, served us steaming hot sweet dark Ceylon tea. It was dusk and red-golden light streamed in through the western window in his office. A black-and-white photo of Mala Mustafa Barzani hung on the southern wall; no other pictures or paintings adorned the white-painted stone walls.

THE DEFIANT

Amin Ismail

Political Prisoner and President, Kurdistan Political Prisoners Union
Interviewed: August 18, 2003

"Kurds believe in justice."

I was in the Kurdish underground, with the resistance, when I was captured in 1982. I had not yet finished secondary school. The Iraqi secret police captured me in Dahuk city on August 24. I was seventeen. It was two o'clock in the morning. Three cars rolled up near my flat. I shared the flat with other underground rebels. There were thirteen of us rebels, in the flat, thirteen with the resistance. Fifteen agents stormed the flat, with pistols and rifles. They crashed the doors and came in from the roof. I suddenly saw them. I woke up and they had their rifles on my neck. They tied a cloth around my head. They tied my hands behind my back. They shouted and screamed at me. The Iraqis killed two and imprisoned the rest of us. They shot our comrades dead right in front of us, with pistols. Under Iraqi law, we had no right to a phone call, or to a lawyer. They blindfolded us and handcuffed us and drove us away. We didn't know it, but we were still in Dahuk. We were eighteen days in Dahuk, and then four months in Kirkuk. After Kirkuk, we went to a special prison for political prisoners in Baghdad, before being taken to Abu Ghraib. Two of my comrades were hanged in Kirkuk. There was no trial.

In Kirkuk, our relatives were able to smuggle in clothes to us. And also, later at Abu Ghraib. The first eighteen days of imprisonment were very arduous. Brutal. We were kept constantly outdoors, in the intense heat, even at night. Our hands were always bound. Blindfolds were kept on us, night and day. You could tell the night from the day in Dahuk by the lessening of the heat on your face. The Iraqi secret police beat us night and day in Dahuk. They beat us with steel cables and heavy wooden clubs.

I knew, then, exactly why we Kurds had been at war with the Iraqis, and why we must win. That is why this time, now, following the defeat of Saddam, means so much to me. We long fought a just and noble cause for Kurdish dignity and freedom. With Saddam still in Baghad, in power, we knew he could return. We knew the hell of Saddam was not over. Finally, Saddam is gone, and he will never return to power. I think of my comrades often, now, and hope their spirits are finally at peace. For they suffered the hell of Saddam, and it killed them. And the first place I really saw Saddam's hell was right here in Dahuk. All the time, we were afraid to eat, or drink water; we knew that would keep us from going to toilet. To go to toilet in the Dahuk prison meant asking a guard, and we'd seen them kill us straightaway, so you had no idea what the guard would do if you asked to go to toilet. In Kirkuk, in the small concrete cells, we'd go to toilet right on the floor. We were constantly ill, in Kirkuk. The Iraqi soldiers would wash their pistols and rifles in our food bowls. The grease, carbon, and dirt from their weapons would always be in our food. It was in Kirkuk that they took off our blindfolds. And they beat us again, over and over.

The torture in Kirkuk was the worst, even worse than we'd seen in Dahuk. All Kurds captured in northern Iraq were sent to Kirkuk. In Kirkuk, the Iraqi secret police used heavy steel fan blades, electricity on your privates, and there was a deep dungeon in the Kirkuk prison. In the dungeon, the Iraqis put a snake near us. They wanted us to fear the snake, and make it angry, so that it would strike out at us and kill us. The Iraqis killed some of us, in this way. The Iraqis also used criminals to beat us, in Kirkuk. The Iraqis had no dignity or sympathy toward us—they were far from humanity.

Many of us were killed in Kirkuk prison by the Iraqi secret police. I bled often from the torture. They broke the legs of many of us. The Iraqis tied my friend to a wall, one evening, and they poured water on him all night. He drowned, standing up. And the Iraqis tried to freeze us to death in the winter. The Iraqis put fans inside the jail, many electric fans. The torture in Kirkuk was constant, unending. I still have scars on my left leg from Kirkuk. One of my friends was badly tortured and hurt terribly. We protested for him to be treated in a hospital. The Iraqi secret police took him to a hospital in Kirkuk and he was treated. Two hours after his treatment had concluded, they took him away and killed him. The Iraqi secret police returned to the Kirkuk prison and boasted, "First we healed him, and then we killed him! Now, he is permanently healed!" They were sadistic, vicious people, the Iraqi secret police. If you have read of the Nazi Gestapo in the Second World War, then you will understand the nature of Saddam Hussein's Ba'athist Iraqi secret police.

At Abu Ghraib prison near Baghdad, the Iraqis continued to oppress us in every way they could. The Iraqis kept us on the rooftop, under a makeshift tin roof, to make it unbearably hot. There was very little food and water—we depended on our visitors. The Iraqis knew that by weakening us, with little food or water, it would exacerbate our illnesses and drive us to death. Some comrades died in this way. We were not allowed to talk in Abu Ghraib. But we talked secretly. Had we been found out, they would've hanged us. And we were not allowed to read.

There were two things that broke my heart. One was when my father came to visit me. The Iraqi secret police had often been forcing accidents on our relatives, to kill them but in a way that they could not be charged with anything. It didn't matter, for the Iraqi secret police could kill anyone in Iraq during Saddam's rule, in truth.

My father along with seven other Kurds were killed by the Iraqi secret police, just after he'd visited me. The prison warden of Abu Ghraib came and told me, in the same hour that it happened, all the time smiling. The second horrifying thing I most remember was the murder of an Arab comrade, right in front of my eyes at Abu Ghraib, right in my cell. He was an intellectual, and a fine poet. He was a good man who believed in freedom for all Iraqis!

One day, the step-brother of Saddam Hussein, Wadban Ibrahim Al Hassan, and three Iraqi soldiers, barged into our cell. They all had AK-47s. Wadban shot my friend three times, in the head. Then the other soldiers opened fire on his body, riddling him with bullets. Some of the bullets ricocheted in the cell. Wadban pointed his rifle at me and shouted, "You have to clap, because we have killed a traitor! Now, clap, clap!" With tears pouring down, I clapped. And they kept their rifles on me, laughing as they jabbed their rifles at me. Finally, they left, and I collapsed on the floor. A guard dragged my friend out of the cell. The Iraqis handed me buckets of water and I washed out the cell. The blood was still on the stone the next day.

Saddam was clever in the way he manipulated the Western journalists, too. We predicted Saddam would release some of us, as if to say to the world that he wasn't as big of a sonofabitch as he'd been made out to be. In truth, he was a far worse sonofabitch than the world ever knew. Saddam did exactly what we predicted. And the Western journalists bought Saddam's game—hook, line, and sinker.

There is a bias in the Western media for Arabs. Consider an embassy reception: the American journalist who, perhaps, is fluent in Arab is discussing Iraqi affairs with an American diplomat who, likewise, is fluent in Arab. The news will reflect both source and reporter, and both in the West have a built-in bias for the Arabs. Take the U.S. State Department, for instance: Ask them how many Kurdish specialists exist. Notice, as we speak: The Americans have no special envoy for Iraqi Kurdistan, even though we stood shoulder to shoulder with the U.S. 10th Group Special Forces and liberated northern Iraq. The State Department Arabists have deep power over the reports the U.S. president receives. Likewise for the CIA; their Arabists are many, and they have terribly limited knowledge of the Kurds. You and the U.S. Special Forces are practically the only Americans I've met who possess any understanding of our history here, and who have apologized for the Kissinger Betrayal of 1975 and the Bush betrayal of 1991. There is no way to reform a dictatorship, you know; you must kill the dictator and drive a stake through the heart of the dictatorship. It was in 1988, then, that a few Kurds were released. No Kurdish Aezzidians were released. Saddam made sure no Aezzidians were released—in this way, he pleased the Arabs, because the Arabization of Kurdish Aezzidian lands had proceeded under Iraqi regimes, prior to Saddam, and Saddam only accelerated the theft of Kurdish Aezzidian tribal lands. The only reason Arabs are in northern Iraq is because Saddam gave them money and property; this is a huge issue, now that Saddam is gone. The only fair thing to do is give the Kurds back their properties and houses, and pay the Arabs reparations for their losses. But now, ecstasy! Saddam is on the run! We must find him and kill him! Ecstasy!

I helped form the Dahuk branch of the Kurdistan Political Prisoners Union on March 6, 2003. With seventeen other former political prisoners, we came together and held our first meeting. We were confident the Americans would crush Saddam's dictatorship. We felt the time was right. Our Dahuk branch supports and supervises eight committees of former Kurdish political prisoners in Akre, Ameydi, Bardarrash, Shingal, Sha h'an, Sumeir, Zakho, and Zumar. Our Dahuk branch also co-ordinates with former Kurdish political prisoners in Mosul. We meet monthly.

Justice. You must know that we Kurds believe in justice. In our uprising of 1991, and in the years since, our peshmerga tracked down and killed some of the Ba'athists who tortured, raped, and murdered our friends, families and comrades. Some of the Ba'athists had stayed in Dahuk, under protection of Tarhar Yaseen Ramazhan and Abdul Kharim Jahayshee. But we found them. We did the right thing. Remember, the Italian partisans tracked down and killed Mussolini. We knew this history, of how the valiant Italian partisans hunted the evil Mussolini. Like the Italian resistance to Mussolini's fascism, we were confident that we could track down the Ba'athist fascists.

And I say this: Let the Kurdish peshmerga join the fight against the Iraqi feydayeen, and against al Qaeda and Al Ansar Islam. We know Mosul far better than the Americans and we can speak Arabic very well. Get the peshmerga in the streetfighting in Baghdad, Mosul, Tikrit, Fallujah, and Ramadi. And attack and attack and attack. We know the borders and the mountains intimately.

THE ORDEAL

Khamel Yaseem Mohammad Dosky

Political prisoner
Interviewed: August 25, 2003

> "There were 800 to 900 Kurdish political
> prisoners when I entered Abu Ghraib in
> 1982. There were six, including myself,
> when I was released in 1988."

I returned to Amin Ismail's Kurdistan Political Prisoners Union office
in Dahuk on August 25, 2003, the fifteenth anniversary of the Gizi
Massacre. There, I met his longtime friend and fellow political prisoner Khamel Yaseem Mohammad Dosky. We talked for a while of
the Gizi Massacre. At one point, Khamel, thirty-nine, rubbed out his
cigarette, frowning, and said, "There is a hatred in Ba'athism for
freedom, for dignity, for justice. There is a fascism at the heart of
Ba'athism that knows no bounds. And it is the silent Ba'athists, the
ones who now claim they knew nothing of Saddam's terror, who
kept Ba'athism functioning in this country, who turned a blind eye—
while our men were beaten to death in the prison right here in
Dahuk. The Ba'athists without blood on their hands, they call themselves, as if the jailer at Auschwitz was no different than the SS
guard. I tell you truly, I know the world was blind to our suffering.
And I tell you truly, we Kurds will never be silenced, now. We have
prevailed over Saddam's Ba'athist terror and we will not be silenced.
Remember Gizi!"

Amin nodded to him and we all sat quiet for a while. A ceiling fan thumped on high, stirring papers stacked on Amin's desk. He set a stone on the papers. Painted on the stone was one word, brushed in wide red strokes: *Halapja.*

■ ■ ■

I was a young man with the Kurdish resistance when the Mukhabarat [Editor's Note: Iraqi secret police] captured me. I was seventeen. I first escaped to Turkey—I thought I'd find refuge in Turkey. But the Turkish Security Forces sold me to the Mukhabarat for money. The Iraqi secret police bought me from the Turkish Security Forces. It was in July 1982. The Mukhabarat in Zakho, on the border, bound my hands, blindfolded me, and took me to Dahuk.

I was tortured in Dahuk for ten days. The Mukhabarat put the electricity on my privates. And they beat me with steel cables, with heavy metal fan blades, with wooden clubs. And with psychological torture, too, they abused me. After those ten days of hell, they blindfolded me and bound me and drove me to Mosul. In Mosul, they took off the blindfolds and unbound me, for a time. For two months, I was in Mosul. The torture continued, but it was more intense. Three of my friends were hanged. I was made to watch them die. Then, the Mukhabarat bound me, blindfolded me, and drove me to Baghdad.

The Mukhabarat held me at a special prison in Baghdad; there were no Iraqi Army soldiers there. It was strictly Mukhabarat. On my first day there, the Mukhabarat stripped me. I was naked. My hands were bound behind me. The Mukhabarat took off my blindfold. And the Mukhabarat put a snake on my body. The snake bit me on my shoulders and legs, and many other places. It must not have been a poisonous snake, for I survived. I collapsed, as the snake was biting me. When I woke up, I was in a cell. My clothes were at my feet. There was no light in the cell. I could hear rats scurrying about.

I was sentenced to death and moved to the political prisoners death row, at Abu Ghraib. I was sentenced to death by hanging. Under Iraqi law, I could not be sentenced to death, because I was seventeen when I was captured. But the Mukhabarat had changed my identity card, to make my date of birth in 1964. So, I was sentenced to death, in this way, like Amin and other comrades. I was kept in a small cell for five months and seventeen days, in solitary confinement. I wish this suffering on no one! When a person tastes pain like this, he wants no one else to taste it. Nothing is worse than to be under political persecution. There were 800 to 900 Kurdish political prisoners when I entered Abu Ghraib in 1982. There were six, including myself, when I was released in 1988. The Mukhabarat and the Iraqi Army killed all the other Kurdish political prisoners.

Twice, the Mukhabarat took me one meter from the scaffold. Blindfolded, with a hood over my head! The rope was ready. They made me reach out with one arm, to feel the hangman's rope. The executioner was there. He grabbed my hood, and leaned toward me, and whispered, "Today you will die, Kurdish pig!" Then, he laughed. I could hear many of them laughing, of the Mukhabarat. I was sure I was going to die. And they grabbed me, and hustled me off the scaffold. Twice, they did this. Twice.

In 1988, I was released, along with other Kurdish Muslim prisoners. The Kurdish Aezzidian prisoners were not released, as Amin told you. That is true. I found out, after my release, that my family in Ameydi had appealed to many people in the Iraqi government, and bribed many Iraqi government officials, to keep me alive. I had no idea, for instance, that the Iraqis had changed my sentence from death by hanging to life in prison, in 1985. What a strange thing life is! For six years, I had waited to die. Yet how mysterious and beautiful life can be! *Kurdi zin duah.*

My God, how fortunate I was that my friends and family were looking out for me, completely unbeknownst to me. How lucky I was. I tell you truly, the joy I feel today, knowing Saddam is gone forever, is a marvelous thing! And my hopes and dreams for the Kurds—I also wish this for all Iraqis. I want the same thing, also, for me and all my family. I want to live freely and I want everyone in Iraq to live freely and achieve their destinies. We have been waiting to be free from Saddam's dictatorship for a long time. Now, that day is here. And we are living the dream of freedom. And this is a beautiful time, a great time to be alive in Iraq.

PROFILE IN COURAGE

Fawsi Muhammad Bawrmarni

Political Prisoner and Director of the Roj Center for Building Democracy
Interviewed: August 5 and 12, 2003

> "What Hitler did to the Jews, Saddam did
> to the Kurds."

Fawsi Muhammad Bawrmarni, forty, is a stocky, solidly-built man,
like a retired middleweight prizefighter, with muscled forearms and
broad shoulders. His eyes are dark and piercing. His skin is sun-
coppered and he is rarely without a smile. A veteran peshmerga in
Hawlerr once told me, "Fawsi Muhammad was valiant for the
revolution; he was a great political organizer, and he never broke
in prison. He carries the spirit of Mala Mustafa Barzani. He is an
honorable man."

Five years ago in Dahuk, Bawrmarni founded the Roj Center for
Building Democracy, which provides training and educational courses
in democracy. Roj Center branches have now spread throughout Iraqi
Kurdistan since the fall of Saddam.

Smartly dressed in blue pleated trousers and khaki short-
sleeved collared shirt, Bawrmarni rolled dark red abacus beads in
his left hand as he talked at length on a variety of topics, some ob-
viously striking a deep, painful, and personal chord. Luckily, when
the conversation ranged to say, the art of Van Gogh and the intrica-
cies of Iraqi politics, his mood lightened as he contemplated Kurdish
future—free, liberated, democratic.

Ah, Van Gogh—from Van Gogh, one learns courage! Truly he was brave, he was defiant in the face of ignorance, he believed in his work. He had the spirit of a peshmerga! Bold to live, bold to stand for his dignity as an artist, bold and uncompromising! We can always learn much good, much that is wise and wonderful, from Van Gogh. He is more alive now, in death, than the Ba'athists ever were in life! Oh, in the hard times, in the difficult times, I would reflect often on Van Gogh's magnificent paintings and my heart would no longer be troubled, I found peace and strength in his art. And now, my torturers are captured, dying, and on the run! Ah, these are days I dreamed of, in solitary confinement, and sentenced to life at Abu Ghraib.

I was with the Kurdish resistance. I was a political organizer for the Peoples Party of Democratic Kurdistan. We co-ordinated with the KDP. I knew Sami Abduh Rahman well; I still know him, and he is now the KDP vice-minister. [Editor's Note: Sami Abduh Rahman was murdered by the Al Ansar suicide bombing in Hawlerr on February 1, 2004.] We were organizing against the Ba'athists, against Saddam's evil. I was captured by Iraqi secret police in November 1986. Six Mukhabarat agents came to my house in Sumeir, with rifles, pistols, and shotguns. They stormed in, breaking down the door. And they blindfolded me, tied my hands behind my back, and drove me to the torture center in Dahuk.

That torture center, by the way, is now the Dahuk University, College of Law and Politics! The place of torture is now a place of learning. This is the good life we know now, where our places of suffering, quite literally, are transformed into places of learning and enlightenment. Enlightenment is a joyous thing, you know.

The solitary was the worst. All solitary is long. The Mukhabarat kept me in solitary confinement in Dahuk torture center for seven months. During that time, they tortured me intensely, around the clock. They flayed my legs until the skin was nothing; blood covered the floor. They broke my hands. They tied electric wires to my ears, privates, and ankles. The electricity was awful. The Mukhabarat used an old phone. The electricity would come on and I'd scream. My eyes would become dark. And the electrical cycle would go on and on and I'd scream and scream. They often tied my hands behind my back and held me from the roof—this was very painful, and I'd scream.

They were always interrogating me, at the same time, trying to get me to break. Trying to get me to give up my comrades, to betray the revolution. But I refused! I refused to betray the spirit of Mala Mustafa Barzani! Oh, the Mukhabarat hated it, if you said the name of Mala Mustafa. That really infuriated the bastards. One of my comrades, under torture, became wild, thrashing about. The Mukhabarat tied him from the roof, and he screamed, "Long live Mala Mustafa Barzani! Long live Massoud Barzani! We live for Barzani! Freedom forever for all Kurds! Freedom forever for Iraq!" And the Mukhabarat beat him savagely but they could not break him.

I often reflected, when I was in solitary, that Kurds share the suffering of the Jewish people. We feel the same pain. What Hitler did to the Jews, Saddam did to the Kurds. Personally, I have great compassion for the Jewish people.

I was brought before an Al Thawla judge, a military judge, after seven months of solitary confinement and torture. The Iraqis brought me a lawyer, who knew nothing about me. The trial was over in a few minutes. The judge sentenced me to life in prison. Life in prison under Saddam is basically a death sentence in itself. Abu Ghraib was a nightmare beyond nightmares. In Abu Ghraib, I saw twelve- and thirteen-year old Kurdish boys tortured until they were forced to say, "I fired an RPG [rocket-propelled grenade] at the Iraqi government." I saw the Iraqis change their identity cards to eighteen years old, and then hang them. These boys were small, just farm boys. Villagers. This was another way for Saddam to murder Kurds. He'd round up the Kurdish boys who were under eighteen, imprison them, torture confessions out of them, and hang them.

And the worst torture was at Abu Ghraib. I saw many of my friends shot dead, killed right in front of me. Arabs, Kurds, Iraqis all—these were good men, brave men, who were simply imprisoned because they chose to fight for freedom in Iraq. They were true intellectuals.

You know, Hemingway had both kinds of courage, moral and physical. His work in Spain, in the Spanish Civil War, proved that. It is good to speak of Hemingway's art. Hemingway was a great innovator. But that is not why I admire him. I admire his courage, his courage as a man and as a writer. He understood that moral courage involves physical courage. One without the other is no good. And the men I knew in prison, they too had both kinds of courage. I will remember them forever.

Many of the prisoners around me were Iraqi Army deserters, from the Iran–Iraq War. They were hanged and shot. There were no rules to the torture at Abu Ghraib. If the guard wanted to beat you, even as you came out of the toilet, he'd beat you. If a guard wanted to shoot you, he'd shoot you. If a guard wanted you hanged, he'd get you hanged. And the guards invented strange, very cruel ways of torturing us. For instance, they forced us to stand on our feet for three hours, watching television. Then, the guards would ask questions about whatever we'd watched. If you could not answer, or answer correctly, they'd beat you on the spot with the heavy wooden clubs and steel cables. This happened every day.

The health conditions were abominable. I was in one huge room, it ran like a hallway. In it, there was a little over 1,000 prisoners. You could only sleep on one side, crunched up. And the Iraqi Army would come to take blood. If you gave blood, you got privileges. Better food, and more water. I told the bastards, "You keep us here for life and you also want our blood! No, I refuse. I will not give you my blood, you've already taken my life!" Oh, the Iraqi guards were without shame.

Saddam was without shame. It was said that before the Iraqi Army would massacre Kurdish villagers and Shia villagers, first, the Iraqi Army medical teams would take their blood. Then, the Iraqis would kill them. I personally saw, in Abu Ghraib, the Iraqis take much blood from prisoners, before they'd hang them. And if you weren't hanged, the food nearly killed you. Abominable. We rarely ate it. I was always thin and weak. They'd give us old rice, with dirt and maggots in it. Rats would drink our soup, before us. My God it was awful.

But luck came my way. My mother visited me! I was so happy to see my mother. I thought she'd cry and wail, seeing me so thin. But she smiled and said to me, "I'm so honored that you're here, because you are fighting the good fight, for our noble and just Kurdish cause." We talked for about an hour. She gave me some food and money. I knew that I was not forgotten. I told my mother that I had gained one positive thing from my prison experience, and it has remained useful, practical even, to this day: The prison was a small Iraq. Abu Ghraib was Iraq, in miniature. You could see many kinds of people, especially politically-motivated people—you could benefit from discussing all political views, from all Iraqi political parties.

Imagine an immense, intense seminar on politics and law, at a college or university, but we kept all of this secret. If our political discussions had been found out, we would've been shot on the spot, or taken to be hanged. We were very, very careful to discuss politics—to talk, at all—when we knew the guards were away.

[Editor's Note: We broke for lunch—hot delicious biriani chicken made with steamed rice, raisins, green peas, onions, red bell peppers, and hot fresh bread with cheese, chilled grapes, orange juice, and hot sweet tea. Following our meal, Fawsi talked about his escape from the Iraqi Army during the Gulf War.]

Before my escape, there were some difficult times, of course, as for all Kurds of my generation. I was released from Abu Ghraib in September 1988; it was Saddam's publicity scam on the West. The Iraqis only released us then because they wanted to distract media attention away from Al Anfal, the chemical attacks. The Western media ate it up.

The Iraqis took us from Abu Ghraib to an Iraqi Army training base. I saw one of my old friends there, a great comrade, and he embraced me and we screamed and cried. After forty-five days, I got seven days leave. But I was refused permission to go home. Then, after the seven days, I was transferred to Shingal military base in the Keskey military area. I spent forty-five more days at Shingal. Then, I went to Sulaymaniyah. The Iraqi Army kept me in Sulaymaniyah until September 1990. The Iraqi Army took me to Kuwait in September 1990. I dug trenches and lived in the sand.

Saddam is a sadist, a torturer. He saw the Kuwaitis as people he could torture, and enjoy it. Of course, he thought he could get away with it. He was a fool. I kept thinking of ways to escape. I thought to get away by requesting leave. So, I contacted an Iraqi Kurdish army officer in Kuwait, and pleaded for leave. He granted it to me, in early January. However, I had to be very careful: My leave papers meant nothing, if the Iraqi Army or Mukhabarat wanted to charge me with desertion, and burn my papers. In Kuwait, we'd heard that north of Kuwait, throughout Iraq, the Mukhabarat was stopping Iraqi soldiers on leave, charging them with desertion, burning their leave papers, and sending them immediately back to Kuwait. So, I dressed like an Arab laborer, in old raggedy clothes, and wore a head covering, like an Arab Muslim. I travelled by bus and I rarely got off it. Always, I rode all night. I rode from Kuwait to Basra, Basra to Baghdad, Baghdad to Mosul, Mosul to Dahuk, and Dahuk to Sumeir. Even in Mosul, once I'd reached northern Iraq, I kept my Arab costume on! Oh, the whole time, I kept my head down and spoke only Arabic. I let my beard grow, too. In this way, I looked very Arabic; the police never questioned me. Thanks to Allah, good luck was with me on my great escape. And how surprised my family was to see me. They cried and whooped for joy!

In March 1991, at the time of the uprising, I'd been married for two years. My wife and I had a one-year old boy. Like many Kurds, we escaped to Turkey at the end of the uprising, at the end of March. We were at the Belaa refugee camp in Turkey. In April, it was raining heavily, night and day. There were twenty days, twenty very long days, in the mud and rain and cold before any relief came. My son died in that time, in those twenty days. I dug a small grave, in an hour and a half. Twenty-two more Kurdish children died, in that hour and a half, in the time it took me to dig my baby's grave. The starvation, the cold, the rain, and the absolute lack of shelter killed many Kurdish refugees, in those twenty days. People were dropping like flies from exposure. My son died from terrible diarrhea, and cold. It snowed, too, and the snow was black. The snow was black from Saddam burning the oil wells in Kuwait.

The Turkish soldiers in the refugee camps were thieves, and their officers were bullies. The Turkish Army stole our food and medicine and sold it on the black market in Ankara and Istanbul, and God knows where else. And the Turkish soldiers didn't hesitate to kill us. Oh, the Turks were brutal to us in the refugee camps. Even after the U.S. Army came, the Turkish Army still didn't care. But the Americans defended us! I even saw an American officer beat Turkish soldiers who were abusing Kurdish refugees. American helicopters came and dropped bread to us. Unfortunately, before the helicopters, there were many air-dropped pallets that did not reach us. And some of the pallets fell on tents, and killed refugees.

It was hardest on my wife, the death of our son. The woman feels this pain more than the man—the mother feels this pain more than the father. I was sad, too, without question. I had many hopes and dreams for my son. But I had seen many sorrows. I'd seen comrades killed right in front of me, in Abu Ghraib. And I knew grief. Like all Kurds of my generation, I'd known grief in a personal way, all my life. I still grieve for my son, as I did when he died. The pain cut deep into my wife's soul. My wife cried all the time, after the death of our son. She was always so sad, always crying. When a woman cries, cry with her. I tried to comfort her, you know, and all of our Kurdish friends and comrades in the camp tried to help her but the pain she felt was so deep, so deep. Many nights, she couldn't sleep, and she'd cry out the name of our son and cry and cry. Sometimes, I'd wake and she'd be gone. I'd follow her tracks in the snow. The prints of her boots, leading from our tent. And I'd find her by the grave of our son. Weeping, in the snow. She would be reaching out, laying her arms on his grave and weeping. Then, I would cry with her, and convince her to come back to the tent before we both froze to death. Oh, it was a terrible time for my wife. Now, we have a daughter. Our daughter will be a teenager, soon. We love our daughter very much. Our great hope is that our daughter never sees the pain and suffering we have seen.

[Editor's Note: During an earlier and separate occasion, we discussed primarily the Kurdish future, radical Islam, the liberation of Iraq, and Middle Eastern politics; that initial interview follows here.]

Democracy is a fire in the Middle East. Not only for Iraq, but for all the region. I think the Arab states would be very wise to realize this. With Iraqis realizing opportunities for travel, investment, and achieving personal dreams which they never imagined in their wildest dreams, they will influence their Arab cousins. You know, we Kurds couldn't even talk to you like this, under the safe haven. We couldn't speak frankly about Saddam's massacres of our people, for instance, as we well knew that the perpetrators were still alive and walking free, under Ba'athist protection, under Saddam's protection. So, already, in just a few short months, the liberation has had enormous effect on my life and the lives of all Kurds and indeed, all Iraqis.

And I think one real meaning of the war is economic liberation. What I mean is that Saddam chained us down, economically. And he gained great wealth by keeping Iraqis impoverished. That is why we have the Big Gap Theory, now very popular among Kurdish intellectuals, very hot. When Iraqi Kurdistan came under the safe haven, and the Americans patrolled the no-fly zone, we Kurds realized we could now open up to the West. We realized we could also manage and plan, direct our lives, without interference and oppression from Baghdad. Thus, for instance, we set up new salary plans and promotions for Kurdish teachers. In 1991 and 1992, economically, we were on a par to the rest of Iraq. Since then, we opened up a huge gap. Our senior professors now enjoy salaries ranging from $125 to $150 in U.S. dollars a month; Iraqi senior professors, even in Baghdad, receive anywhere from $10 to $35 a month. You can imagine how difficult it was for Iraqi teachers to care for their families, under Saddam's oppression. But that will change now, of course.

There is a Big Gap between Iraqi Kurdistan and the rest of Iraq, and it is not only economic, it is cultural. We have strengthened our cultural identity in these last twelve years of quasi-autonomy. Our children have renewed their pride in Kurdish culture and fewer of them speak Arabic, as compared to my generation. My generation was forced to learn Arabic; we do not put the same chains on our children, it is a choice for them, not an obligation enforced by a dictator. And our artists, for instance, are seeking international exhibitions abroad, in Europe and America and Asia. Our artists know that the West welcomes their contributions to world culture. Our artists, like Seerwan Shakkurr and so many fine Kurdish artists, deeply understand and recognize that the West welcomes freedom of expression. So, our ties as Kurds, extend first to Europe and America, not to the Arab world. And that, too, makes for a Big Gap. We have much more in common, in our thoughts and ideas, with Europeans and Americans than with Arabs.

The very notion of freedom, the very idea of democracy, which we cherish dearly and teach our children to value and treasure— these are Western ideas, not Middle Eastern ideas. And there is a deep bond now between Kurds and Americans, an emotional bond, a bond born in blood and sacrifice. We bled with you. We crossed mountains with you, we fought alongside you, we lost our warriors in a common cause. So, our initial impulse, when we see an American, is to thank him and welcome him, not to curse him or vilify him.

We Kurds are living in a glorious time, because it was Saddam Hussein who said, "The Kurds are ignorant about self-government; they don't need autonomy because they are savages and barbarians." Who is the barbarian, now? Ah, Saddam is a beast on the run and I hope the Americans capture him and strike him dead. But the threat is real from al Qaeda and Al Ansar Islam, from all radical Islamic terrorists. They are in love with death.

Kurdish intelligence knew that al Qaeda was being supported by Saddam Hussein, long before the Americans asserted it. Radical Islam in the Middle East, and Indonesia and the Philippines, is the source of terrorism. I am a Muslim and I say to you, radical Islam has nothing to do with Islam, nothing at all. Radical Islam is a blasphemy against all true Muslims. The thoughts of Arabs must change, and there is so much poverty in Arab countries. And Arabs must first look to themselves and seek the changes within their own cultures if they are going to end the endemic poverty in their countries. And this is why the war to liberate Iraq is so very important. America, by liberating Iraq from dictatorship, liberates the Iraqi people from poverty and unending lack of opportunity.

You see, the young man who has opportunity, hope and bread on his table will not have a thought for Osama bin Laden, or any other radical Islamic terrorist. The central problem with radical Islam lies with Islamic extremist mullahs, in the madrassas, in some of the Islamic schools. That is the heart of the problem, because that is where poor Muslim youths get their introduction to the Koran and their basic schooling. But if all they learn is hatred of the West, if all they learn is how to hate Americans and Westerners, they simply become hate machines on two feet. And that is a tragedy, for the mullahs have stolen their youth from them and really, stolen their lives. Islamic extremists are blind people. They never see clearly and they cannot appreciate any point of view, other than that of radical Islam.

My duty, as an educated man, is to help the poor by teaching them the beauty of freedom and informing them that as a human being, they possess inalienable rights which no one has the right to deprive them of: the right to life, freedom of speech and expression, education, and health care, these I consider inalienable rights. Radical Islam, of course, believes in no such thing. And radical Islam preaches hatred of real education, when you get right down to it. But America is with us, thank God. And America understands, I believe, that its very own survival is at stake in the War on Terror. The survival of freedom and dignity for Kurds is also at stake in the War on Terror. And I tell you, we did not prevail over Saddam's horror only to fall victim to the horror of radical Islam. No, we shall overcome the radical Islamic terrorists, and we will help America in every way, to gain victory over the fascism and evil of al Qaeda and all who stand with al Qaeda. We will prevail over evil!

There is great envy of us Kurds that's been fired at us from all directions. The Turks, Persians, and Arabs have always envied our love of independence and freedom and our wealth of resources. Also, we enjoy natural resources, such as water, oil, and timber, that the Turks and Arabs have always tried to steal from us. And there is the cultural issue. We are surrounded by cultures younger than us, and they envy us for our ancient culture.

The original Kurds, Kurdish Aezziddians, have kept our core Kurdish culture alive for more than 6,000 years in this region. When you see a Kurdish Aezziddian religious dance, which is a very joyous and moving celebration of the gift of life, you are witnessing it exactly as it was performed 6,000 years ago. None of the neighboring cultures can say this. *Kurdi zin duah.*

So, I think envy has a lot to do with it. Arabs, Turks, and Persians have tried to destroy Kurdish civilization, in order to supplant it with their own. But they failed! The spirit of Mala Mustafa Barzani is the true Kurdish spirit, the undying love of liberty, dignity, and honor. That instinctive love of freedom is not shared by other Middle Eastern cultures, and they hate us for holding on dearly to our love of freedom, they detest us and disrespect us, for this reason.

We have democratic foundations in Kurdish culture. Our women can walk our streets with our men. They can study in the same classroom. They can own and manage banks. They can start businesses and drive cars, and like Jula Hajee, lead all Kurdish women to teach all Kurds to respect women's rights. Jula Hajee is a great leader for our women. [Editor's Note: See page 117.] Our women can walk without headwraps, that is their right. Our human rights of women are well-protected and the dignity of women is intact in Kurdish culture. Yet look at women's rights in radical Islamic cultures. Look at the Taliban's rule in Afghanistan and the influence and power of Wahabist Islam in Saudi Arabia. My God, the Taliban was killing women just because they walked to a market on their own. Beheading women in front of crowds, for this "crime." And we Kurds, unlike the Saudis, for instance, do not believe in denying women their rights and privileges. Even in Iran, if someone sees a woman's hair, she is scolded and whipped for this "offense."

What crime is it to Allah that a woman's hair is seen? If God created women, he created their hair, too, that is beyond all argument. The laws denying women their freedom in the Middle East are cultural and tribal—they do not come from Allah. There is nothing in the Koran, by the way, that says a woman must be a walking blanket, completely covered up. So, other Middle Eastern cultures, especially Arabs, disrespect us for this reason, also. They disrespect us because we treat our women differently than they do; they detest the fact that our women have the right to choose to wear a headwrap, or not. And we Kurds accept, and exploit, the changes which technology has made in our lives and in the lives of all people, in our generation. But there is an innate Arab refusal, finally, to accept the reality that technology has irrevocably changed our world—changed the way we do business with one another, the way we travel, the way we communicate. Arabs, and all Middle Easterners, must understand that it is impossible for them to control the world. The radical Islamists actually believe this lie, that they will control the world because they look back at the lands conquered by the Prophet Muhammad and say this time will come again. It is a vain quest. If they do not give up this idea, they will either self-destruct or be destroyed. As the ancient saying goes, "Pride goeth before the fall."

The Arabs are holding on to their old history because it is a time they take great pride in. But all they really have is their pride, as a result. If you are constantly beating your chest, living full of pride and wallowing in pride, you will stagnate and choke yourself in your ego and delusions. Pride is a very dangerous thing, and no pun intended, nothing to be proud of! You must look to the future, not the past. The future is our children's time, it is the unseen "now" we can build by helping our children's generation, in our lives.

I see the road ahead for the Kurds, in liberated Iraq, as best if we separate from Iraq. The Kurds were pasted to the Arabs with British glue and the expiration date on that glue vanished a long time ago. But that time is not quite now, for a free and independent Kurdistan; now is the time to help Iraqis build a democratic, federal Iraq. I say that we should form our own country, between five and ten years from now, because Kurdish culture is so completely different than Arab culture. And I see the road ahead for Kurds as one that is shared by Americans, God willing. We see Americans as our friends. We bled with you to slay the dragon! No one can ever take that away from us.

The great thing in Kurdish society since 1997 is that we are unified. Our troubles, our civil war, are over. All Kurdish tribes contributed to the war to free Iraq, without disputes or in-fighting. That is a degree of unity which is unprecedented in Kurdish history. And the fact that radical Islam is a presence in Syria and a strong influence on Turkish politics does nothing to help build democracy in Iraq. The Islamic party in Turkey is controlling a great deal of Turkish affairs, and that is not positive for the U.S. especially with Turkey being a NATO member.

THE MASS GRAVES AT HATRA

Specialist Eric Debault and Lieutenant Colonel
Randal Campbell

U.S. Army 101st Airborne, U.S. Army Investigators
Interviewed: August 2, 2003; July 29, 2003.

> "There were so many skeletons. Layers
> of victims."

Specialist Eric Debault

Specialist Eric Debault, twenty-eight, speaks seldomly and when he
does, chooses his words with care and precision. Slim and reserved,
he has the direct, clipped speech of a Midwesterner and his nick-
name is "The Quiet Man." His short-cropped blond hair, in the paratrooper style, befits his presence in the elite U.S. Army 101st
Airborne Division (Air Assault). The 101st was heavily engaged in actions against the Taliban and al Qaeda in Afghanistan, before slugging
it out from Kuwait to Mosul in the war to liberate Iraq. Much of Iraqi
Kurdistan fell under the 101st command, and they operated several
liaison offices with the Kurds. Specialist Debault was with the
Peshmerga LNO in Dahuk when he journeyed to Kurdish mass
graves at Hatra, 120 kilometers southwest of Mosul, as part of a doc-
umentation and investigation team of the 101st. In the operations
center of the Peshmerga LNO in Dahuk, Debault lit up a smoke and
nodded. I pulled out my notebook.

■　■　■

I saw a baby skull. I will never forget it. I saw a baby skull with a bullet hole in the back of the skull. There was a forensics specialist on site. He was an American, with the 101st. His name was Dr. Rodriguez. He held the baby skull in his hands. He told us it was, at most, a two-month-old baby who had been murdered. I just couldn't imagine how somebody could extinguish all the warmth and humanity in their heart and get so evil that they could look in the eyes of crying women and children, begging for their lives, and put a rifle to their heads and smile and squeeze the trigger. How can you do that? How can anyone do that? To just murder people in cold blood? The vast majority of the people in those graves were women and children. Women and children.

You can see what Saddam was doing. It flashed in my mind like a lightning bolt at Hatra, in the sands. Right there, I knew Saddam perpetrated genocide against the Kurds. That alone was reason to destroy his government. Saddam was murdering the Kurdish hope, the future: women and children. That would've wiped out the Kurds, forever.

I detest the United Nations for their greed and their cowardice, for refusing to back the war. I want to make that very clear. Gutless bureaucrats and diplomats of the U.N. Cowards. No moral courage. No backbone. Their own resolutions were violated, and Saddam was the worst weapon of mass destruction Iraq has ever seen. And only God knows how many Kurds Saddam murdered, how many Kurds Chemical Ali murdered. But they will never murder Kurds, again, no! That's not going to happen! And in the desert, at the mass graves, I reflected on how the Kurds feel about the Iraqis, how the Kurds find it difficult to trust Iraqis. And I understand, 100 percent how the Kurds feel about the Iraqis, now. I really do. The Kurds are a very knowledgeable people, a people with a great culture and history. A very respectable people, and they have treated me with utmost respect and courtesy. Anything that the Kurds would want to do to the Ba'athists, to Saddam's fascists, is entirely justifiable.

Americans have no idea of the horror Saddam perpetrated; but he will never perpetrate it again, against the Shias or Kurds or Sunnis. Really, Americans, and the world, have no idea of the horror I have seen. All this was on my mind, standing there in the desert, looking at the skulls and bones. I would consider Saddam as the Anti-Christ. Saddam is the very personification of evil. Saddam ranks right up there with Hitler, Stalin, Mussolini—with every brutal dictator who has ever carried out crimes against humanity.

■　　■　　■

Lieutenant Colonel Randal Campbell

Lieutenant Colonel Randal Campbell, forty-four, is passionate about his wife, his family, and the 101st, in that order. He stands just over six feet tall and is heavily muscled. He's seemingly always grinning, and rarely without a cup of coffee in hand. He first served in the U.S. Army as an enlisted man and rose to Sergeant, before heading on to OCS (Officer's Commissioning School). The Missourian studied history for his B.A., and he later earned a Master's in Political Science. A graduate of U.S. Army Ranger School, Air Assault School, and Airborne School, he wore the Combat Infantryman's Badge.

The 101st discovered the mass graves at Hatra, in the first place, from tips from Iraqi Arab farmers. Iraqi Arab farmers led us to them. You could see, immediately, that there was something wrong with the ground. There was no grass over the site, any flowers, just very bare flat ground that looked like it'd been packed down, hard and flat. There was no change in terrain, or vegetation, not the slightest, the barest dip in the ground or hint of a weed or flower. It was just a huge circle of barren ground—vegetation began at the edge of the circle, in all directions. And this is only one of the six mass grave sites at Hatra, by the way. The Kurdish peshmerga were very helpful, at this early stage, and throughout the ongoing investigations. The pesh-merga used their Arabic, and conversed at length with our Iraqi informants. Based on the information from our informants, I reckoned that there were six different mass graves.

I gave the 101st ten-digit grids for each mass grave. We dug twice. On the first dig, the Iraqi and Kurdish guides were unsure and they didn't follow the intelligence. They didn't dig according to the grid points. They only dug down about two feet, with shovels, and found nothing. I ordered a second dig, with an excavator. First, the excavator dug down about four feet. Still, we found nothing. So I ordered him to dig down at least six feet. He dug down just over six feet and we found layers and layers of skeletons, skulls, bones—my God! It was horrifying. You saw it and you knew Saddam's genocide against the Kurds, his crimes against humanity, are all too real.

On the first day, we pulled out twenty bodies. By the third day, we'd pulled out eighty-seven bodies. Dr. Bill Rodriguez, our forensics specialist, is a certified forensics pathologist. He determined the sex and age of the victims. There were so many skeletons. Layers of victims. The Iraqi Army must have laid the corpses up in stacks. The Kurds have always said that many families were disappeared. That, for instance, they'd hear trucks drive away in the night. Whole Kurdish villages, and the people would never be heard from again. Hatra is where the Iraqi Army and the Mukhabarat took the Kurdish families, I am sure. All of the ghosts Saddam tried to hide will reveal themselves, in the days and months and years to come. What goes around, comes around. Saddam killed 182,000 Kurds in Al Anfal.

Where did he disappear the bodies? We are finding out now, exactly where he buried the bodies. You know, it was the 101st that liberated some of the first concentration camps, in Nazi Germany. And here we are, nearly sixty years later, liberating another country from a brutal fascist dictator. And discovering the evidence of Saddam's horror, as we found out just how evil Hitler was, on another continent, in another era. The nature of man does not change. The nature of evil does not change, just as the nature of good does not change. The Iraqis near Hatra, the Arab farmers, had varying ideas on the number of Kurds buried there. Captured Iraqi intelligence agents, under interrogation, have told us that it will be well over 10,000. Well over 10,000 Kurds murdered and buried in the mass graves at Hatra.

The Ba'athists knew no shame and they loved to kill Kurds, they loved to murder anyone who wanted to live free and live without fear. And those days are gone and they are not coming back. Ba'athist fascism is finished in Iraq, and it is on its last legs in all of the Middle East, for that matter. In all my years in the U.S. Army, I have never felt prouder than now. I know exactly why we came and why our mission, to free Iraq from Saddam Hussein's Ba'athist dictatorship, is so right, so necessary. I really feel like I'm doing something important.

THE KILLING FIELDS

Faisal Rostinki Dosky

Director, KDP Intelligence
Interviewed: August 12, 2003

> "The U.N. is doing nothing to aid the investiga-
> tion of war crimes and mass graves in Iraq!"

At the KDP Intelligence Headquarters in Dahuk, its director, Faisal
Rostinki Dosky, punctuates his remarks with a lit cigarette, sipping
tea as his conversational points sink their way into the minds of two
bodyguards, a translator, and myself. Bright-eyed and baldheaded,
Faisal is a calm, thoughtful man who is a native of the Dosky tribe, a
tribe that was very active in the Revolution of 1961. Nearly every
Dosky I met in Iraqi Kurdistan was either active-duty or retired peshmerga. The villages of Sindoor and Nazarkhay are solid with the Dosky
tribe, as is the city of Dahuk itself.

■　■　■

After Operation Iraqi Freedom, we started to collect a lot of information from our contacts in the south. The intelligence my agents collected was very intriguing. It confirmed my own thoughts, over the
years, of many Kurds being driven off into the desert and massacred.
All Kurds were well aware of this.

Our people in the south, after the fall of Baghdad on April 9,
2003, interviewed many Iraqi Arabs. Arabic is a second language for

nearly all Kurds, and we gathered massive amounts of information about the location of mass graves in Hatra, mostly from Iraqi Arab farmers. They were very helpful in this way.

What convinced me was the consistency. Our intelligence network got consistent information on the existence of Kurdish mass graves at Hatra. All the information was pointing to the same place. I was sure, after reviewing the collected intelligence, that the Iraqi Army and Mukhabarat had massacred Kurds at Hatra.

In the second week of June, I visited the site and I saw some signs, just looking at the ground, that were very strange. For instance, there was a huge circle of undisturbed ground. Barren, hard, flat ground, not like a desert with small clumps of sand and small roots and flowers. Very strange. Also, insects were burrowing straight down and coming straight back up.

We made contact with Coalition forces and we informed both sides of our investigation into possible Kurdish mass graves at Hatra. The Americans reacted enthusiastically. They pulled an investigating team together, including the forensics pathologist Dr. Rodriguez, and we set a date of July 3 to begin a joint investigation. The Americans interviewed our sources, also. After confirming our intelligence, the Americans told me that they were convinced there was a Kurdish mass graves site at Hatra. They took great pains to assure us that our human intelligence had been very helpful to them. The entire mass graves site, by the way, is within a ten-kilometer grid square. Thus far, only one of the mass graves has been dug up.

It was a sight that I will never forget. To see the skeletons of so many of my people. My people have suffered horribly. Saddam targeted us at Halapja and Gizi and Soriya, in the torture centers and the mass graves at Hatra.

You know, the Iraqi Army lieutenant, Abdul Kharim Jahayshee, who perpetrated the Soriya Massacre just north of Dahuk in 1969, was kept well-protected by the Ba'athists for many years and is reported to be in Mosul. Yet he walks free, and he led the murder of thirty-eight Kurdish Chaldean Catholics and Muslims at Soriya on August 16, 1969. The evil in the heart of Lieutenant Abdul Kharim is the same evil in the hearts of the Iraqi Army soldiers and officers, and no doubt, Mukhabarat, who killed my people at Hatra. Jahayshee received a double-jump promotion, in one day, for murdering Kurds at Soriya. That was a standard Ba'athist procedure, by the way. Ba'athist military officers who led massacres of Kurds and Shias were promoted, on the same day, up two grades. Lieutenant Abdul Kharim Jahayshee went from First Lieutenant to Major, in one day, for leading the massacre at Soriya.

I looked at the skeletons in the pit, stacked in columns, and I knew that evil is real, that hell is a living thing. There is a hell inside Saddam that knows no limit. He and Chemical Ali, especially, were in love with evil. Now, we know.

Unfortunately, the investigation of the mass graves at Hatra had to be postponed, due to lack of funding. But it's not only funding. There has been a great lack of international co-operation. Where is the United Nations on this matter? The U.N. has only proven that it manages problems, and does not solve them. The U.N. is doing nothing to aid the investigation of war crimes and mass graves in Iraq! Where are the Germans, with the lessons of their own Holocaust?

Due to the lack of international co-operation and funding, we have, quite reluctantly, postponed the ongoing investigations into the Hatra killing fields. Iraqi Army intelligence officers, whom we and the Americans have captured and questioned, believe that there are at least 10,000 Kurds massacred and buried in the mass graves at Hatra.

THE SORIYA MASSACRE OF 1969
Adam Yo Nan and Noah Adam Yo Nan

Chaldean Survivors

> "My father was also under the bodies, with
> my sister. I was drenched in blood. I thought
> they were dead."

Infamous among Kurds and largely unknown otherwise, the Soriya
Massacre of 1969 was orchestrated by Abdul Kharim Jahayshee, a
confidante of the prominent Ba'athist Tarhar Yaseen Ramazhan, who
made the infamous Most-Wanted List of fifty-five headed by Saddam.
[Editor's Note: Ramazhan was captured in Mosul by Kurdish peshmerga in a brilliant raid on August 20, 2003, who handed him over to
the 101st Airborne on the same day.]

I spoke with several survivors—a father and his adult son—of the
Soriya Massacre. Adam Yo Nan is a Kurdish Chaldean Catholic who
was born in the Kurdish Chaldean Catholic village of Arboli, Turkey, in
1921. As a young boy, he moved to Soriya, northern Iraq—a Chaldean
Catholic and Kurdish Muslim village. He now lives in Dahuk, northern
Iraq, with his wife, daughter, and son, Noah, who was born in Soriya
in 1959. Noah is married, with two children. Adam's daughter never
fully recovered from the massacre.

I met Adam and Noah in their ancient stone house near the ruins of
a church on the western reaches of Dahuk on a beautiful late September
day. President Ablahadd Sawa, leader of the Chaldean Democratic
Union, who had fought for years to get the story of the Soriya Massacre

told internationally, had joined us, sitting back gravely on a wooden chair. He wore a dark blue suit, button-down white shirt, and a gold tie. He has known Adam all his life, emphasizing, "There were only a few survivors at Soriya and we have done all we could, all these years, to both protect them and to get their story told. Adam has told me many times that the horror of that day must never be forgotten, for that would only increase the Ba'athist terror—and the Ba'athists are still out there."

Noah is a tall, fairly slim man with an easy-going manner and a very strong handshake. His father, Adam, is shorter, with eyes like Hemingway's Santiago in *The Old Man and the Sea,* undefeated eyes that are cheerful and full of hope.

■   ■   ■

Adam

No other writer has ever talked to us about the Soriya Massacre, the day that ruined my daughter's life. I was sitting in a room after Mass. I was in a house, near the village headman's house. Near the front of the village. I was talking with a visitor from Turkey. It was our Holy Day, a Sunday. The 16th of August, 1969. We heard an explosion. We knew it was an anti-tank mine. The KDP peshmerga had been planting anti-tank mines on the main road, from Zakho to Dahuk, to ambush the Iraqis. I remember my friend, from Turkey, telling me it sounded like it had come from the road junction area. Our village was the closest one to this road junction. About seven kilometers from the road. Our village headman was not lazy. He went out to the road, quickly, and came back. He told us the anti-tank mine had disabled an Iraqi troop truck. He said there were no casualties, and he directed everyone to go inside, into their homes. Then, I could hear the low rumble of truck engines, nearing our village. I went outside. Eight Iraqi Army troop trucks were entering our village, dust trailing in clouds behind them. It was a hot, dusty day. Each truck carried twelve soldiers. No one in our village was armed. The Iraqis carried revolvers, Kalashnikovs, and machine guns.

Noah

It was Sunday. We'd come back from Mass. My father talked with the village headman, after the explosion. We always had Mass on Sunday, and our priest was there, in the village with us. Father Hanna Kasha was our priest.

Adam

The Iraqi Army ordered us all together, collecting us at gunpoint in a small garden, in front of a house. They waved their Kalashnikovs at us. There were Muslims living with us, in our village, and many of them had already run away, when they'd seen the trucks entering our village.

Noah

First, Iraqi Army First Lieutenant Abdul Kharim Jahayshee shouted, "Where are you hiding the peshmerga, where are they?" The priest said, "Please talk with me and let the women and children go back to their houses." Our village headman stood with the priest, and pleaded with Lieutenant Abdul Kharim to let the women and children go. And both of them told Lieutenant Abdul Kharim, "If you want something, we will provide it for you. But please let our women and children go." Lieutenant Abdul Kharim raised his Kalashnikov and shot our village headman. Then, he shot the priest. We all screamed. Children grabbed their parents. Everyone was wailing and screaming.

Adam

And I will never forget the courage of the village headman's daughter. She was truly brave. Her name was Layla. She attacked

Lieutenant Abdul Kharim, with her bare hands. She grabbed the Kalashnikov from Abdul Kharim and had it leveled on him but another Iraqi soldier opened fire on her and killed her. Then, Abdul Kharim pulled the rifle from her dead hands and opened fire on all of us, on automatic. I saw him change magazines. They were the curved magazines that hold thirty rounds. I saw him put his third cartridge in, and shooting from the hip, waving his rifle at us as he mowed us down.

Noah

I was ten years old and I fell on the ground. A woman fell over me and her blood covered me. Other children, too, were covered in blood and thought dead. At the same time, the Iraqi Army soldiers in our village began spreading out, shooting into houses and burning the houses. Then, Lieutenant Abdul Kharim led the destruction of the village. As he did this, two Iraqi Army soldiers, who were Kurdish, spoke Kurdish and Chaldean to us—they leaned over the mass of dead bodies and spoke to us, saying, "Anyone who is alive, try to escape. If Abdul Kharim comes back, he will kill you all. Escape now."

My father was also under the bodies, with my sister. I was drenched in blood. I thought they were dead; I did not know my father was alive. It was too dangerous to speak. I saw my mother and we ran away. While we were running, wounded people escaping with us died of their gunshot wounds, bleeding to death. We were all running to the village of Bakhlogia, four kilometers away, to hide. We got to Bakhlogia but the villagers couldn't give us refuge; it was too dangerous. So, we ran to another Christian village, Av Zarook.

Adam

I was too scared to run away. I had my baby daughter in my arms. I panicked and couldn't move. It was like my legs were made of lead. My daughter was six months old. [Editor's Note: Adam paused for perhaps three or four minutes, then breathed out deeply, grimacing, and continued.] The time of the massacre was 9:30 A.M. on that Sunday morning. There was a wooden fence around the small garden. Lieutenant Abdul Kharim came back from leading the destruction of the village, after he'd shot us, and he ordered his soldiers to bend the fence around us.

We were just a mound of bodies. I was covered in blood. I could see another lieutenant, a Second Lieutenant, who said to Lieutenant Abdul Kharim, "Do not shoot these people. You are mad! There has been enough blood, for one day. Do not shoot these people." And Lieutenant Abdul Kharim smiled at him, the smile of a shark as it is feasting, and replied, "Be quiet and shut up. Otherwise, I will kill you."

Abdul Kharim, by the way, is a member of the Ba'athist party. It has been the Ba'athist party that has protected him all these years. I held my baby in my arms the entire day. At six P.M., after all was quiet, I took my daughter and went to Av Zarook—all of our relatives were in that village. She cried and cried! Oh, she screamed when Lieutenant Abdul Kharim killed our village headman. I had to cover her mouth with my hand, to keep her quiet. I was afraid she'd suffocate. She was very angry, and her fists were clenched hard. That night, she cried all night. All night, and into the next day. So many of us were wounded and crying.

My daughter went mad from the Soriya Massacre. She was a normal, thriving baby before that. She would laugh and talk baby talk and play with her baby toys. Since that day, she has been insane. She cannot stand the sight of strangers, for instance. When she was one year old, we took her to the doctor. He told us that she had gone insane.

The majority of our wounded went to Mosul. I went with them. No doctor would see us. We were not allowed in the hospitals. The Iraqis refused to admit us. Just admitting us to the hospital would've acknowledged that the Iraqi Army had slaughtered us. You should know, and the world must know, that Lieutenant Abdul Kharim Jahayshee was very proud of leading the Soriya Massacre.

Noah

Lieutenant Abdul Kharim Jahayshee sent a telegram directly to Saddam Hussein in Baghdad. The telegram read: "I have killed many peshmerga at Soriya." And he asked the Ba'athist party to send an order to all hospitals in Mosul, and Dahuk province, not to accept any wounded Kurdish Chaldean Catholics or Kurdish Muslims from Soriya and the surrounding villages. Abdul Kharim Jahayshee was promoted to major in the Iraqi Army directly after the Soriya massacre. He became a protégé of Tarhar Yaseen Ramazhan, who established the Al Jaesh Al Shabee, a second army for Saddam in northern Iraq, and enlisted people up to forty-five years old during the Iran–Iraq War. Abdul Kharim was very helpful to Tarhar Yaseen Ramazhan, and was promoted to Dahuk Commander of the Al Jaesh Al Shabee. He held this position up to 1989. Abdul Kharim is believed to be living in Mosul. The Ba'athist loyalists, no doubt, are taking very good care of him. We must capture him and kill him.

[Editor's Note: While a war correspondent with snipers and scouts of the 101st in fall 2003, in Mosul, I presented the preceding evidence from survivors of the Soriya Massacre, as a war crimes report, to the 101st. Nothing was done. Later, after returning from Fallujah in mid-February 2004, I again presented the same report to Task Force Olympia, which had replaced the 101st. Again, nothing was done.]

AL ANFAL GENOCIDAL ATTACKS ON THE KURDS

Hajee Omar Sharif and Issa Hajee

Witnesses
Interviewed: August 13, 2003

> "The Iraqi Army put us in big holes in the
> ground. There were 300 to 400 people in
> each big hole."

Saddam's genocidal campaign against Kurds was called "Al Anfal,"
which means "The Great Battle Against Non-Believers" in Arabic. The
phrase Al Anfal comes directly from the Koran. Saddam Hussein was
trying to appeal to all Muslims to believe that his genocidal operations
against the Kurds were justified by the Koran, when he named his
most brutal reign of terror, "Al Anfal." The terror began in fall 1987 and
continued until fall 1988. Al Anfal resulted in the deaths of 182,000
Kurds and the exodus of nearly all Iraqi Kurds to abominable conditions
in Ba'athist concentration camps in Iraq and to Turkish refugee camps.
The most vicious and brutal one-day killing by the Ba'athists during Al
Anfal was the infamous Halapja bombing, where the Iraqi Air Force
dropped chemical bombs on Halapja, killing 5,000 Kurds in one day.

In a stone-walled courtyard on the northern edge of Dahuk, an
ancient man who was a survivor of Al Anfal sat across from me.
While remembering when the British used mounted horses to po-
lice Dahuk in the 1920s, the conversation quickly focused on
Saddam Hussein's chemical attacks and bombings of his village,
Satarngay, in 1988. Satarngay is south of Sumeir, and is roughly fifteen

kilometers west of Dahuk. Rolling wheatfields blanket the plains west and south of Satarngay.

The gentleman's name was Hajee Omar Sharif and he was eighty years old. He was spry and his gaze was clear and steady. We shook hands and he motioned to a seat, next to a translator. With Hajee was an old friend, Issa Hajee, sixty-eight, from Beskay village, near Satarngay.

■ ■ ■

Hajee Omar Sharif

I was born in 1923 in Satarngay. At that time, it was a nice place. The British came, now and then. They gave us little trouble; it was the Arabs, even then, who were trying to steal our land. Six times in my life, my land has been stolen by Arabs—we lost everything, each time. Six times, we have regained it.

The worst, of course, was Al Anfal.

During Al Anfal, we were imprisoned at Bayharke, like the people of Gizi and so many Kurds. My village was destroyed by Saddam Hussein's Iraqi Army—once, he personally came to my village and oversaw the destruction. In Al Anfal, I lost my brother, son, and son-in-law.

The Iraqi jets bombed us with the chemical death in Al Anfal. First, the airplanes came and bombed us with chemical weapons. Also, I saw them bomb Zinevah village. We escaped—those of us who survived—by walking through the mountains. But the Iraqi Army surrounded us in the night. They arrested us, and tied all the men's hands behind their backs. They stole all our possessions. And they took us to De Hay, a Christian village. In De Hay, the Iraqis put tanks in front of us. We were sure we were going to be massacred. It was August 1988. But they did not fire at us. They made us stand in front of the tanks for the longest time, and then they laughed at us.

Then, we were moved to Circinck, for only a day. We were very thirsty, hungry, and tired. We got no food or water. Then, they brought us to Nzarkay Castle [Dahuk prison]. For three days, they held us at Dahuk prison. The Iraqi secret police came, and separated the men from the women and children. And they tortured everyone! They tortured the men, and boys over ten years of age, the most.

Nobody could dare talk. They beat us with iron bars, stones, concrete blocks, and wooden clubs. There was no food and no water, for three days. No one could sleep—we were so afraid. The men were taken in blacked-out cars. You could not see in, through the windows. The cars returned, after three hours. The cars returned without our men.

I was judged too old to kill, so they did not drive me away. They took me, with all the women and children of our village, to Salamiyah. Over the coming years, with freedom in Iraq now a reality, Kurdish skeletons will appear all over northern Iraq. Already, they are finding the mass graves at Hatra and Hilla. Salamiyah was hell. Like all Al Anfal. All Kurdistan was hell, and Saddam was the Devil incarnate. The Iraqi Army put us in big holes in the ground. There were 300 to 400 people in each big hole. We had no toilets. There was very little food or water, and no shelter. Many of our people died daily, from dysentery and cholera and exposure. Especially the young children, and the babies. We didn't dare even look at the Iraqi soldiers or they'd torture us. After a month in the killing pit, we were moved to Bayharke. That is where I met the survivors of other massacres, such as the Gizi survivors. We were put in an open area behind barbed wire. No one could visit us, not even our relatives. The Iraqi Army surrounded us. Here, in the Bayharke prison, I met my old friend Issa Hajee. I was so shocked to see him! I was sure he'd died in Al Anfal.

Issa Hajee
It was a terrible time in Bayharke. But our Kurdish people were still able to smuggle in food, medicine, and blankets. People even smuggled in tents and plastic sheets. The summers were brutal, under

the plastic sheets. In the winters, we had no heaters and sometimes, no blankets—the men were always giving up their blankets to the children and women. We lived in canvas tents, in the winters. Normally, five to six people died each day from exposure, diarrhea, cholera, and in the summer, heat stroke. And this was just in one small sector of the entire prison.

From my village of Beskay, twenty four of our men were taken and killed, even before we got to Bayharke. My village, Beskay, is near Zawita. Like Hajee Omar Sharif, the Iraqis first took us to Dahuk Prison for three days of torture, and then took all the men away and murdered them. I was just as shocked to see him as he was to see me! I was sure the Iraqi Army had killed him. It was hell on earth, Al Anfal. Hell on earth.

Hajee Omar Sharif

But we are happy to be alive, now, with the fall of Saddam! Death to Ba'athism! Oh, April 9, 2003, was a grand and glorious day! We were together, on this day, with our wives! And we raised our hands and thanked Allah! Oh, Allah be praised! We are free from Saddam's pestilence, from his damnation!

We thanked God that America released us from the terrorist Saddam. For many years, we prayed to Allah for this to happen. It brings me joy, just thinking of that day. We both hope and pray that all Kurds live free forever, from this day forward. And we must capture Saddam. He must die, for what he has done. Kill Saddam! April 9 will always be a sacred and divine day for Kurds. And we hope that America stands by us.

Please don't leave us alone. America is our last best hope. I am sure that all Kurds share my feeling, my hope, and my dream that America stands with us, for a long time.

THE UNDERGROUND

Three Anonymous Members of the Syrian Kurdish Underground

Interviewed: August 13, 2003

"We will live free or die."

In Dahuk, I met three resistance operatives with the Syrian Kurdish Underground. The men were each given a made-up nom de guerre for reasons of personal safety to protect them from the long and bloody reach of Syria's Ba'athist fascist dictatorship. Convinced they were being tailed by Syrian Ba'athist secret police even here in Iraq, they requested that our interview be brief.

■   ■   ■

Jamil

The Syrians are no different than other Ba'athists; they seek to destroy the identity of anyone who disagrees with them, anyone who is not first Arab. Ba'athism destroyed Iraq, it is easy to see that now. Ba'athism continues to cause Kurdish suffering in Syria. For example, the Syrian Ba'athists stole my land and put Arab families on it. I still have the original documents proving that I own the land, but it doesn't matter. If I asked for my rights, or even raised the issue, I'd go to jail for life or be killed.

Moussa

Kurds have no rights. We are not allowed to study at university. And we were forbidden, previously, to even raise our voices in Iraq, because of the Ba'athist brotherhood between Saddam and the Syrian dictator, whose son is now just as much a dictator as his father.

Muhammad

I make one point: the Kurds in Syria are hoping that the Iraqi Kurds develop and gain independence. And the Iraqi Kurds and Syrian Kurds are tribal relatives. We are not forgotten by our Kurdish brothers. There is a reason we are able to meet you here, you see. And we seek the liberation of Syrian Kurds. If we cannot gain freedom in Syria, we will flee here. It is madness, in Syria. For example, examine my ID card. It reads that I am a Syrian Arab. That is the only way I could get it. You cannot identify yourself as a Kurd, in Syria. In only one of our Kurdish cities in Syria, Amir, which is half the size of Dahuk, 150,000 Kurds have disappeared since the 1960s.

Moussa

Anyone who asks about them, anyone who raises this issue of the murder and disappearance of Syrian Kurds, is also arrested and never seen again. The Syrian Interior Ministry and their Ba'athist secret police are just as brutal and vicious to Kurds as Saddam Hussein's Mukhabarat was to Kurds in Iraq.

Jamil

All the oil and farming income in Syria comes from Kurdish land. And the Syrians have always sought to deny us our land, as a result. The National Security Laws discriminate heavily against Kurds. We have no rights in Syria, none. Unless we change our identity to Arab. And even then, we only have the rights of Syrian Arabs, which do not include freedom of speech, press, or any human rights. The Ba'athist dictatorship in Syria is a callous and evil regime.

Yet the United Nations recognizes it, adores its diplomats, and finds no reason to chastise it! Tell me, what good is the United Nations?

Inside Syria, the secret police make Kurds register with them if they stay overnight in a town or city. And if you are travelling with your wife, and you are Kurdish, you cannot sleep in the same room with her. The Ba'athists even oppress us in this way, by keeping us from sharing the company of our women.

Muhammad

We Kurds are not allowed to participate in politics in Syria, at all. Not even at the village level. But as my comrades have said, all the oil money and agricultural revenue comes from Kurdish land. Fifteen per cent of all Syrians are Kurds. But not one minister, not one government official, and not one ambassador or foreign ministry official in Syria is Kurdish.

Moussa

There is a sign in Arabic in the Interior Ministry: It reads, "There is nobody called Kurd in Syria." This year, Kurdish children demonstrated in Damascus, at the UNICEF center office because they thought it was at a U.N. office. The Ba'athist secret police would not dare to halt the demostration. It was a silent protest. One of the children gave a flower to a Syrian policeman. The policeman beat the girl, refused the flower, and arrested seven of the children. The United Nations have made no mention of this.

Muhammad

Jamil and Moussa are my comrades and they have spoken truly of our oppression. I want you to know that we do not believe, and nothing we've seen in our lives can convince us otherwise, that there is a diplomatic solution to ending Ba'athist fascist dictatorship in Syria. Just like there was no diplomatic solution to ending Ba'athist terror in Iraq. Fascism is the same, everywhere, and must be rooted out and destroyed.

Our last solution is war. We are prepared to fight as guerrilla fighters, as peshmerga, but we are not yet organized. We only ask that all Kurds in Syria enjoy the rights guaranteed under the United Nations Charter on Human Rights. But if the U.N. cannot honor its own charter, we will not wait for our deliverance. All men are born to be free. And we will live free or die.

Book Three:

The Road Ahead

WOMEN'S RIGHTS

Jula Hajee

President, Dahuk Branch: Kurdistan Women's Union
Interviewed: August 6, 2003

"I must honor our war widows."

The Kurdistan Women's Union commands a fine view of mountains south of Dahuk that rise like the Kurdish spirit, indomitable. Ironically, the building is but a stone's throw from Saddam's former Iraqi Army base. Across the street is another symbol of the Kurdish yearning for liberty and dignity—the Lalesh Center for Kurdish Aezziddians. These days, Dahuk's streets are filled with optimism and joy, two emotions quite at home in the heart of Ms. Jula Hajee, who is the president of the Dahuk Branch of Kurdistan Women's Union. Born in 1974 in Sumeir, Iraqi Kurdistan, Hajee is famous for her efforts to defend Kurdish women's rights. Pleasant, charming, easy-going, and full of energy, she is petite, with classic Kurdish woman's looks: bold, bright eyes, and high-cheekbones. She wore a long-sleeved flower-print dress, of an indigo background. Her staff, including a translator, came in as tea was served. Fawsi Mohammad Bawmarni then entered the room, to great acclaim. He coordinates job training intiatives with Hajee.

■　■　■

I joined the Kurdistan Women's Union in 1998. In 2001, I was elected president of the Dahuk branch, which covers all of Dahuk province, to the Turkish border, the Iranian border, and south to Mosul. We have eight branches in Dahuk region, throughout northern Kurdistan. We are making three new branches, right now, in Baghdad, Kirkuk, and Mosul.

We started some projects for widows because we have so many war widows, and they learn how to help their families. I must honor our war widows. The world must know the pain Saddam caused our women in Kurdistan. The world must know. There is so much poverty among Kurds, because of the destruction of Saddam. Perhaps the most troubling and long term effect of Saddam's genocide against Kurds has been the psychological torments and maladies, especially among women who lost their families to Al Anfal. Also, our women, who were raped or tortured by the Mukhabarat and the Iraqi Army, suffer terribly, from psychological problems. Saddam's forces gave nothing but horror to the Kurds, and our women continue to suffer from the memory of his horrifying regime.

Without their husbands, who died valiantly for our just and noble cause, our Kurdish widows are lonely, and loneliness can easily breed depression. The aim of the project to aid widows is to get jobs for women, so they can support their families and re-build their lives. So our women feel they have reasons to continue living. One of the programs within our widows project is our sheep distribution program. We distribute sheep to needy families. In 270 villages, thus far, we've distributed 13,000 sheep to 2,300 families. This is an excellent program and we will expand it! It provides widows with wool, mutton, and money.

Ah! I must tell you of our young Kurdish women in this program. They are young and clever. Twelve young Kurdish women manage the sheep distribution program. They created the project, by the way. This is an excellent job-training program for them, too. It provides them with many management skills. As with all our programs, the overall goal of this project is to help women make progress econom-ically, socially, and in health care.

We are teaching Kurdish women how to have healthy pregnan-cies. This is our women's birthing project, to improve the health of Kurdish babies and their mothers. For many years, we've wanted to lower our infant mortality rate. One reason Kurdish women, even today, have had so many children is that they knew they'd lose some of their babies, due to poor nutrition and general lack of medicines and supplements. Our women's birthing project aims to give solid, sound health education to mothers of all ages. Already, we have 760 young women working on this project, throughout northern Kurdis-tan. We are having great success with this project and will continue to expand it, to reach out to all Kurdish women and help them have healthy pregnancies.

We've also started a beekeeping project, with the help of the World Food Program. The WFP gave us 100 beekeeping kits and also information on how Kurdish women could become independ-ent businesswomen, by getting the bees to make honey. I thought it was a splendid idea. I pulled together some of our young women and they planned the project. Then, they went out into the villages of northern Kurdistan and began training Kurdish women in how to be-come beekeepers. Again, we've been fortunate to have great success with this project and we look forward to teaching this skill, which makes money and honey, to more Kurdish women.

Also, I must say we've had very good coordination with Mr. Fawsi Mohammad, of the Roj Center for Building Democracy, especially on job training projects, such as computer courses, seamstress and tailoring, small business training, health courses, Kurdish culture courses, literacy, music, dance, and physical fitness.

It was on November 12, 1952, that we began our long journey. That was when the Kurdistan Women's Union was founded for women's rights. Our first meeting was in Baghdad. Baghdad has a large Kurdish community, you know—approximately one million Kurds.

Kurdish women have never been afraid to speak out on issues concerning Kurdish human rights, dignity and freedom for all Kurds. In 1952, we had many Kurdish women in the peshmerga, working in the Kurdish underground. Many Kurdish women were also working behind the scenes, in politics, at that time. And, as you may know, some Kurdish women fought with peshmerga. Margaret is our most famous Kurdish woman peshmerga. She was Christian and she was beloved. She died fighting the Iraqi regime. Oh, she was a brave woman and she was very loyal to Mala Mustafa Barzani. I will never forget Margaret. The Kurdish people, especially Kurdish women, keep her in our hearts, forever.

One of our great Kurdish heroines is Nahida, the mother of Dr. Roush, who is himself today a leader among Kurds. Nahida is very brave, and a brilliant woman. Nahida is still alive today, in Hawlerr. One hundred years before Nahida stood in Baghdad at our first conference, as far back as 1852, there was scholarship on Kurdish women, on their importance to Kurdish culture, that was published in *Das Ausland* magazine in Stuttgart, Germany. So, I am fortunate, today, that I can build on a long foundation of bravery of Kurdish women, fighting for Kurdish dignity and women's rights, thanks to the sacrifices of so many Kurdish women who came before me, like Nahida and Margaret and so many unsung heroines, who made it possible for me to help Kurdish women today, in our time.

THE ARTIST
Seerwan Shakkurr

Painter and Teacher
Interviewed: August 10, 2003

> "Under Saddam, to exhibit one's work
> outside of Iraq was forbidden."

Art lives and breathes in the personality of Seerwan Shakkurr, who is one of the most respected artists in Iraqi Kurdistan, and indeed, in all of Iraq. Generous, gregarious, and exultant are apt labels for the thirty-five-year-old internationally known painter. With a firm handshake and smile, he welcomed me into the shaded quiet of the Sculpture Garden at the Dahuk Institute of Fine Arts, in Dahuk. He was nattily dressed in a single-breasted gray tropical-weight suit and gold tie. His translator walked up to us a few minutes later, apologizing for being tardy. As is the custom with virtually all guests, tea was served and cigarettes were passed around.

Married with two small daughters, his home is a tribute to art, filled with his own landscape paintings as well as paintings and sculptures from Kurdish artists. He's been teaching painting and sculpture at the Dahuk Institute of Fine Arts since 1992. His art was smuggled out of Iraq, during the dictatorship of Saddam Hussein, and met with increasing success in European and Asian galleries. "Now I no longer have to smuggle my paintings through the mountains into Turkey!," he said with great elation. "Saddam is gone! Hurray!"

■   ■   ■

I graduated from the Baghdad College of Fine Arts in 1990. After the safe haven was established in Northern Iraq in 1991, no one was allowed to go to Baghdad to study. No worries. We established our own institutes of fine arts.We are Kurds and we have a long, long tradition in the arts. We have three colleges of fine arts, now. In Sulaymaniyah, Hawlerr, and here in Dahuk. We teach design, plastic arts [Editor's Note: painting and sculpture], dance, theater, audio-visual, and music.

You must know this. Under Saddam, to exhibit one's work outside of Iraq was forbidden. He wasn't keen on Kurds painting, or for that matter, living. But I got my work smuggled outside of Iraq. And I've been fortunate to have my work shown in exhibitions in Denmark, Germany, and Japan. *Kurdi zin duah!*

I began painting quite young. Drawing and sketching first, of course. When I was a young boy, I'd go fishing all the time. I loved the outdoors and all of nature. So, I began painting nature. Even then, I was very enthusiastic about painting. I have always loved to paint. My brothers would go fishing with me, too. They are in Denmark and Germany, now. My sister is here in Iraqi Kurdistan. She is a veterinarian, and married to my good friend, Kawa of Hawlerr.

Kawa and I, like all Kurds, faced many dangers during the Ba'athist terror. Saddam's secret police, the Mukhabarat, would place Ba'athist spies in the classrooms at all Iraqi universities. The evil Mukhabarat! They were Gestapo! This happened to all Kurds at Baghdad College of Fine Arts. And throughout Iraq, at all colleges and universities.The key was not to talk about politics. All Kurdish students had a Ba'athist monitor, but you didn't know exactly who your monitor was, who was the spy. It could be someone you thought was your friend. You could not confide your political thoughts to anyone — we had to be very, very careful. In that sense, the university was like a jail. Sometimes, you could tell who Saddam's spies were. For instance, there was an Iraqi Arab art student I remember from my second year of studies. He was always scowling, this man. He never seemed happy. He came right up to me, after I'd finished a canvas, and began arguing that the Palestinians will all go to heaven and the Israelis will all go to hell. He asked me if I agreed.

I told him I only know that Jackson Pollack is in heaven and art critics are in hell, and he walked away, muttering under his breath. I knew, right away, that he was a Ba'athist spy, this student. I stayed away from him, the rest of my studies. I told all my friends, of course, to keep their distance from him, too. Only a spy for Saddam, and a not-so-clever spy, at that, would say such a thing to a Kurd at an Iraqi college.

Ah, I must honor Michaelangelo and Picasso! Long live Michaelangelo and Picasso! When I came to preparatory school, I finally began to really study Michaelangelo and Picasso. I'd long heard of them, of course. I was always lucky to have good art teachers in Kurdistan. Michaelangelo and Picasso, absolutely, remain my greatest teachers, my main influences. Their art inspired me in my youth and continues to inspire me, and to shape and inform my work. Michaelangelo's Sistine Chapel murals really, really moved me. His vision was vast and broad, his skills were so well-honed, and he was, of course, quite gifted. What a marvelous artist Michaelangelo is. Kurdish artists say there is no sculptor superior to Michaelangelo. Well, God is a better sculptor than Michaelangelo. You see the hand of God in these Kurdish mountains and you know that God is a magnificent sculptor.

And I like Picasso very much, also. I adore Picasso's wit and his daring. His iron sculptures are very exotic. Picasso was a man of open ideas. How interesting his paintings are, how fascinating they are. He was always challenging himself. You can always see, even in his early work in Barcelona, an artist who is passionate about the craft, a man who knows his calling. Picasso was also a man of great sexual appetites.

His eyes wandered to many flowers, and women were greatly attracted to him, as well. It is a fact that women are attracted to artists. Women are instinctively drawn to beauty, and thus to creators of beauty.

You know, we teach the masters, such as Michaelangelo and Picasso, differently here, due to lack of money—we can't afford text-books, for example. However, we have many posters of the master works, and our professors have great knowledge of the masters. So, we lecture, and relate our experience and ideas in our lectures. We want our students to be open-minded, and active-minded—not only about art, but about all society. Artists are part of society, and can only grow if they are engaged in the issues of their generation.

Our students say, "If you want to do something, you can do it. If you don't, you can't. You must desire to achieve. Without desire, life is mere existence." It was our desire to honor Kurdish dignity and freedom that emboldened our brave peshmerga, and led to the safe haven years, and now, liberation.

Because Iraqi Kurdistan enjoyed the safe haven, we could set up a separate pay system for our art teachers, for all Kurdish schools, of course. Here it is much better than Baghdad. The Dahuk city government, and Dahuk regional government, have done a lot for Kurdish painters. The salary is much higher, here. At first, we received four U.S. dollars a month; that was in the first year of the safe haven. Then, in 1992, it was increased to eight dollars a month. Now, a first year art professor receives sixty dollars a month. And that is under review for an increase. I started at four dollars a month, and now receive one hundred twenty-five dollars a month. My wife is very happy with my salary. *Balleyyt*.

And I also sell my paintings. From one exhibition, overseas, I received slightly over $1,000. From another, just over $1,200. The gallery owners did great work, selling my paintings. It is a great feeling, to know that people from another culture appreciate your work. And the shadow of fear from Saddam is gone forever!

And my students will live free from the Ba'athist evil, forever! Oh, my students are exultant, now! Yes, my students are well. You know, I always tell my students that if I graduate one student a year who loves art, then I will be happy. Of course, we graduate far more than that.

My students have been flowing in to see me, all summer, since the fall of Saddam. They are very enthusiastic about their futures, now, with the downfall of Saddam's dictatorship. Many of them have exclaimed their thanks to America and the Coalition.

Each year, we bring in one hundred sixty new students—eighty girls, and eighty boys. We begin with the basics, the foundation of plastic arts—painting and sculpture. We have eighty degrees each year, for drawing, twenty degrees for art history, and thirty-six in plastic arts. I always talk to the first year students, personally. They must understand that they have twenty-one absences, only. Over twenty-one absences, and they are expelled. I tell them that they are responsible for their projects, and that their projects determine their grades. In their fourth year, I will counsel the really sharp students personally, and help them in every way. I encourage them, in this way, to become great artists.

It is very important for older artists with experience and knowledge to encourage and support the young artists. It can make a difference in their lives. The older artists did this for me, when I was their age; it is a pleasure to carry on the tradition.

And for my family, I have one wish. For my daughter, who is blind. She was very sick, in her brain, with physical illness. The doctors told us that there is a very small part of her brain that affects her sight. And this minute part of her brain is very bad. She cannot see. My dream is that she can go abroad for an operation and see, one day. That she can see.

And for me personally, I want to show my work in more international exhibitions. The new airport at Sulaymaniyah could really help, in this way. With Saddam gone, I can now travel wherever I want. This is a huge difference in our lives, for all Kurds. We have a freedom that we never had before, thanks to America and the Coalition. For Kurds, I want a state, an independent state. That is my hope and my dream. All Kurds in their hearts want an independent state. And a good life. Where we don't think only about money, but about developed humanity, also. A good life, with science and art and human rights. A good life, with security. With freedom from terror. And good relations with all of our neighbors. These are my hopes and dreams. And I must always honor Michaelangelo and Picasso. Long live Michaelangelo and Picasso!

ARTISTIC DREAMS AND THE LONELY FIRE
Nasim

Kurdish artist
Interviewed: August 16, 2003

"Van Gogh was valiant, like our peshmerga."

Nasim is a young man, barely out of his teens, bursting with all the passion, ambition, and conviction of a naturally born artist. His skin is dark from the sun and his eyes are brown. He stands just over six feet tall, and is casually dressed—T-shirt, jeans, and boots. He was the top student at the Dahuk Institute of Fine Arts, before graduating in 2003. He paints in several styles: realistic, surrealistic, and excellent portraits, rich with emotion and feeling. Van Gogh is his hero.

I met with Nasim in the sculpture garden of the Dahuk Institute of Fine Arts. Dusk was falling, and he delighted in pointing out a flock of starlings swooping and darting over the courtyard. He also enthused about other romantically inspired topics—women, Aphrodite, and his longing to paint the Colombian singer Shakira. "Her curves are classical, as if shaped by Michaelangelo."

■　■　■

In my youth in Dahuk, I stayed with my grandmother and grandfather. Dahuk was empty and full of ghosts. We lived in fear of Saddam. Dahuk was very dirty, too, and the streets were always full of garbage.

I tell you, I always loved to draw and paint. I never had to conceptualize my love of art. It was just there. I feel very fortunate, in that way. My gift is also my calling. I think it was your Thoreau, the American philosopher, who said, "Most men live lives of quiet desperation." But I am not one of those men.

In primary school, I began to paint formally. This was my introduction to art, in a serious sense. The other boys would ask me, "What will you be?" And I would always answer, "I am an artist." They would laugh, and say, "No! How do you already know who you are, you are just a boy!" And I would tell them, "I love art and I love to paint and draw. I know I am an artist. I am an artist!" The little girls would smile at me, when I would say this. That is when I first knew that women adore art.

We had very few supplies, and even in secondary school, we had few resources. But I could draw, of course, without spending much money. It is not difficult to find materials, if you do not give up. You must not give up, that is the vital thing. You only need pencil and paper, or charcoal and a rock. The rawness, the richness and wonder of the cave paintings in France and Spain come from this truth, that the artists had absolutely no regard for money—the work is pure, from the boulevard of the heart. All great art has this purity, this truth. I seek this purity.

I graduated from this institute in June 2003, after the liberation. And Van Gogh and Picasso, they are my greatest teachers, their art inspires me! Professor Seerwan taught us to respect and honor the masters. Thanks to him, I discovered the joy and majesty of Van Gogh. I am very much influenced by the life of Van Gogh. He worked so much but nobody cared. Yet he followed his road. He was valiant, like our peshmerga, our guerrilla fighters, in Kurdish highlands. The world was silent to our suffering, yet our peshmerga followed the road of freedom and dignity for all Kurds. How brave! That is Van Gogh's bravery, his boldness, his daring. In the face of ignorance and ridicule, he dared to listen to his heart and follow his solitary road. His heart was compassionate, you can feel it in his art. And in Van Gogh's art, I feel a yearning fire. The fire never dies, no matter how often I see his work. The lonely fire. The fire that burns with infinite power—it can never be extinguished. How brave he was, to follow his road. We follow him now into eternity. He did so much, he was such a creative genius, he left such treasure for all the world to adore. His style of brushwork, his bold new style, opened new emotions in art. He was truly daring and truly dedicated. I feel spiritual depths in Van Gogh, deep spiritual depths. I think Van Gogh's emotions guided his brush.

And I must not forget Picasso. I like Picasso because he was a very active man, in all aspects of his life. He did not separate his art from his life. Everything in his life affected his art. He changed his style, so many times. He never stayed in one style, even though that would've made it easier to sell his work. Picasso was always, always challenging himself. This is a great lesson for all artists. Every student must challenge himself, to really develop as an artist. Without challenge and struggle, there is no change within. And it is the inner journey that leads to the outer journey.

Now, I am teaching art at a juvenile prison—the Juvenile Reform Centre (JRC), here in Dahuk. I'm living with my father and he is buying my supplies and material for me, thank God—they cannot pay me at JRC. I am painting new work, day by day. I am planning, now, to open an exhibition abroad. My aunt is making contacts for me in Europe.

The interpretation of Islam, by some people, makes it difficult for artists. Religion is a difficulty however, even in Kurdistan. Some Muslims, especially radical fundamentalists, say, "Whoever paints a man or woman goes to hell!" This is garbage talk, of course. But it hurts our society, and damages all the Muslim world. This may lessen, of course, with the great victory of April 9.

We have many roads of opportunity opening for us, thanks to the Americans and the British and all the Coalition. These roads are two-way roads, which will expose our people to the wonders and beauties of Michaelangelo, Picasso, Van Gogh, Pollack, and so many other great artists of the West. And I think this is a good thing, a great thing. This is a beautiful time to be alive, *Kurdi zin duah!* To this day, we feel this joy at the end of Saddam's dictatorship. We dreamed of this day for many years. Now the dream is real. Even my uncle, who was a Kurdish general in the Iraqi Army, felt the fear of Saddam in his life. Saddam's dictatorship burned my uncle's house in Basra in 1997. And they kept him under observation, always. He was never free to go to the market, and never free to travel. Finally, he escaped to Turkey in 2000. Always, the Mukhabarat shadowed him. Oh, he is happy now, too!

And for my people, I hope democracy lasts forever for us. Our human rights must never be compromised. The great struggle of the Kurdish generations before us, the many sacrifices and the horrible suffering endured, must be honored by my generation. We will honor the path of Mala Mustafa Barzani in our work and in our lives. The freedom we enjoy today is born of the bravery and struggle and sacrifice of our peshmerga. Our Revolution was not in vain, that truth is alive today in the freedom we breathe.

And for myself, as an artist, I want to make a new name in art, especially in painting. I want to honor the great foundations in art which the masters, like Van Gogh and Picasso, forged so brilliantly. I seek to honor that greatness in my life, in my work. We must dream big dreams. I want to always strive, to be honest to myself, to not betray my integrity as an artist. I know this will be difficult—it has already been difficult—but there is joy in the journey when it comes from the heart! I have been fortunate to listen to, and to learn from, fantastic artists like Seerwan Shakkurr. Our artists in Kurdistan possess great knowledge and great talent; it is a blessing to learn from them. Our roots as Kurdish artists are very deep. They go back for ages and ages. I hope that all Kurds never forget the contributions Kurdish artists have made to our culture, our society. And I want to blaze new trails as an artist, in Kurdistan and all the world.

SCULPTOR
Nazar Mahmoud Othman

Professor of Ceramics, Dahuk Institute of Fine Arts
Interviewed: August 20, 2003

> "During Al Anfal, I was heartbroken and dev-
> astated. I was very sad. I could not express
> my sadness and my misery, even in my art."

I spent a bright, sun-splashed summer morning on the rooftop, which overlooked the sculpture garden at the Dahuk Institute of Fine Arts, sipping tea with Nazar Mahmoud Othman, Professor of Ceramics. Unlike most Kurds who refrain from saying anything untoward or impolite, Nazar Mahmoud Othman, thirty-eight, likes to joke around. But just minutes earlier, we had heard from fellow instructor Seerwan Shakkurr that Tarhar Yaseen Ramazhan, a prominent Ba'athist and mentor of Abdul Kharim Jahayshee, perpetrator of the Soriya Massacre, had been captured in a daring daylight raid in the heart of Mosul by Kurdish peshmerga.

■　　■　　■

It was quite difficult, being an artist under the long shadow of Saddam's dictatorship. Saddam's spies were everywhere. I studied in Baghdad, for six years, from 1985 to 1991. When I was a freshman, in 1985, the older Kurdish students warned me about Saddam's monitors. They told me to never, never get into a political conversation, and to avoid all talk of Kurdish culture, entirely. I was extremely careful. They were right. The Ba'athists spies were everywhere. Sometimes, another student, or even a professor, would ask me a political question. Always in a studio or classroom. I'd never answer.

I'm also a musician. I play the aoud and the barzakk. I began playing when I was a boy, before I was ten years old, and began singing and performing when I was fifteen. And the girls would come around and listen. I liked that, very much. As I got older, however, I wanted to teach art. And I also loved sculpture and ceramics. I still play the aoud, and barzakk, to please my wife. I always sing for her, too, to bring her joy.

But I began in ceramics. That is my start, as an artist and teacher. At the Baghdad College of Fine Arts, I had an excellent advisor and teacher, Professor Marhar Samarahayy. He earned a Masters in Fine Arts in New York City. He was a wonderful teacher, very encouraging and supportive, with a hard critical eye.

I must also honor Pablo Picasso and Leonardo Da Vinci. Picasso was very dynamic, very bold and daring. He absorbed many cultures in his work. He was always learning, always growing. The marvelous African art, for instance, is very much alive in Picasso's work. The merging in his art, of Europe and Africa, builds a wonderful bridge between cultures. You know, Picasso was never afraid to fail! Perhaps that is why he flew so high. Picasso still flies high, for that matter. His art has soared over all the mountains of the world. Indeed, Picasso has soared beyond time; his art endures. I must say, I have learned much from Picasso, and from his early work in Barcelona. The soul of Spain is always in Picasso's work, that deep Spanish soul you hear in flamenco. When I see Picasso's work, I hear flamenco.

And Da Vinci, such an artist. What a wealth of artists Italy has given the world: Da Vinci, Michaelangelo, Caravaggio and so many others. And Dante, of course, who painted with words. Da Vinci's technical skills are unparalleled, to this day. His mastery of classical art is profound—it is a joy to see his work! You can hand an apprentice artist just one of Da Vinci's sketches, a mere sketch by the great Da Vinci, and he will learn everything he needs to know about art, all the fundamentals. Da Vinci knew line like an eagle knows sky. His knowledge and understanding of line are striking, vivid, and unsurpassed. And the great Da Vinci must be honored for his lovely, touching and profound masterpiece, *Mona Lisa*. What a testament to Da Vinci that poems have been written for *Mona Lisa*, that songs have hailed the beauty of *Mona Lisa*. His *Mona Lisa* can never be exhausted—it never tires the eye, it never tires the soul. There is a mystery within the smile of *Mona Lisa* which is truly beyond all words. That is the touchstone of all great art: the mystery that is truly without words. You can read Homer all your life and never lose the joy of reading him, the delight in his verses. [Editor's Note: Nazar went quiet suddenly, and he winced. Something was troubling him. After a few minutes, he glanced up.]

You know, I was in Baghdad, during Al Anfal. I was heartbroken and devastated. I was very sad, during Al Anfal. But I could not express my sadness and my misery, even in my art. I prayed for my people, night and day. I prayed that Kurds would survive this tragedy and live to see the defeat of Saddam. We were in a prison in Iraq, all of us, a prison of silence. I thank the Americans and British for liberating us from that prison of Saddam, and giving us the chance to break the silence. And I tell you, what joy I felt to see Saddam's statue fall. Death to the dictator! We were overjoyed, My wife held me close and our children gathered around us and we were very, very happy. Oh, the joy and contentment, knowing that the evil Saddam has fallen from power! This was our big dream, you see, for so many years. And we dream that Ba'athist fascism never returns to power in Iraq, indeed, that it has no place whatsoever in Iraq's future. Saddam caused so many people to suffer. He starved the Shias and ruined their marshes. He destroyed their way of life, and nearly destroyed Shia culture. He killed anyone who believed in freedom for Iraq. His henchmen, like Chemical Ali and Tarhar Yaseen Ramazhan, were truly brutal. They were his Gestapo and they were utterly and completely ruthless. To know, now, that they are captured and will be brought to justice, it is difficult for me to really express how happy that makes me feel. For my family, I wish long life and happiness and I hope my children live free from the horror which my generation suffered under the Ba'athist dictatorship of Saddam. And I must say, for myself, I want to be a famous artist. And to introduce young artists, who will do great work. For my people, for all Kurds, we must take our new rights, so that we can make a democratic, federal Iraqi Kurdistan. And I want every Kurd in the world to enjoy their human rights.

"HELL IS OVER. AND WE HAVE AMERICA TO THANK FOR THAT!"
Kawa Fathi Massom

Attorney
Interviewed: August 10, 2003

> "I can say, with a whole heart, with my
> soul at peace, that now, my children, you
> have a future."

I waited with Kawa Fathi Massom, forty-four, for the translator to arrive at the sculpture garden at Dahuk Institute of Fine Arts. Kawa wore a white short-sleeved shirt and khaki trousers and a perpetual grin. He is a broad-chested, stocky man. Gray and silver streaks color his dark hair. A graduate of the Ministry of Technical Mining in Basra, in 1977, his real passion has been human rights law, since his youth. At the end of the internecine fighting between the KDP and PUK, in 1996, he graduated from the College of Law, in Hawlerr. He practices law in Hawlerr and Dahuk, and works in the main Court of Hawlerr. He is married, with two young daughters. The prestigious Kurdish artist Seerwan Shakkurr is his brother-in-law. Our interview began with a memorable anecdote.

■　■　■

Yes, it's true. I met the great Mala Mustafa Barzani when I was six months old. I was just a wee small baby. Mala Mustafa took some hair from his son Massoud's head, and put it on mine. Then, Mala Mustafa patted me on my head. And he said, "May God save you." My family witnessed this and told me later, when they knew I'd remember. Mala Mustafa is our George Washington, he boldly fought for our freedom and our dignity. Mala Mustafa remains our hero, our guiding star. We will never forget his struggle, his vision, and his sacrifice. His spirit still guides us. He was a visionary, and yet, very much a man of the people. He never forgot the common man, he never looked down on the rank-and-file guerrilla fighters of the peshmerga.

I know there is some talk in America, now, that America and the Coalition should not have liberated Iraq. That Operation Iraqi Freedom is a huge mistake, and that America will be bogged down here in an endless war without purpose, to no end. I want Americans to know this, what I say now. I want all the world to know this. All my life, when my four sons and my daughter would ask me, "Daddy, do we have a future? What will be our future in Iraq, Daddy?," I lied. I was not an honest father to my children, all my life. Until now. Before April 9, 2003, I never felt certain, not at all, that my children would live with freedom. I always lied to them and told them that, of course, they'd have a good future with dignity and liberty, and opportunities to achieve their dreams. But I was lying, and it killed me inside, I often talked with my wife about this, and she told me that there was nothing else I could really say to our children. To tell them the truth would break their young hearts. For the truth is that as long as Saddam Hussein remained in power, with his brutal Ba'athist dictatorship intact, no Iraqi had any hope of a real future. And certainly not the Kurds, my people. The safe haven secured Saddam's safety far more than it ensured Kurdish safety.

President George W. Bush finally realized that and acted on it; the United Nations only served to protect a brutal dictatorship, not to end it. I thank God President Bush and Prime Minister Blair are real men, men whose moral compasses are not malfunctioning. And they both understand that freedom is never free, as we Kurds have understood it all our lives. This is the almighty difference the Americans have made in my life: I am a father to my children, an honest father to them! Truly it is an almighty, almighty difference in my life, and my family's lives, and I am eternally grateful to the brave American soldiers for liberating the Kurds, and all Iraq, from the horror of Saddam. I can now live as an honest father to my children, for the rest of my life! Oh, I cried on April 9, 2003, I wept. My wife and children hugged me. My daughter asked me, "Daddy, why are you crying?" And I looked in the eyes of my children and I told them that all their lives, I'd lied to them. That I'd always told them they'd have promising futures but that I knew I was lying and I hated myself for that. And now, now, I told them, I could not lie. I can say, with a whole heart, with my soul at peace, that now, my children, you have a future, and we have the Americans to thank for this. My wife says that I am like a new man; she is so kind and lovely, my wife. She kept me strong, in all the dark years, in our time of suffering and damnation. And America freed us from Saddam's damnation. So, I am sorry but I do not understand Americans who protest and criticize this glorious war to liberate Iraq from one of the most brutal dictators in history. As long as Saddam Hussein continued to rule in Iraq, the entire region was under the shadow of fear—Saddam is a madman, he is a cruel vicious barbarian who must be captured and killed. And there are still Ba'athist renegades and Saddam loyalists who wish nothing but harm to the Americans and Coalition forces.

I hate to see any American soldiers killed. There is a small, intense, and well-funded resistance, the feydayeen. The feydayeen can be defeated and annihilated, if America listens well to the Kurds and to the Iraqis. Human intelligence is absolutely crucial to destroying the feydayeen. Al Qaeda and Al Ansar Islamic terrorists were supported by Saddam, also, and they maintain links to the Ba'athist renegades— they maintain links to the feydayeen. That is no surprise to the Kurds.

America won the main battles. Now it must win the counter-guerrilla war. And the Kurds will not hesitate to help American soldiers win the counter-guerrilla war, if given the chance. And I understand the pain Americans must feel. But consider the pain America will feel if it loses Iraq and this country becomes a base for al Qaeda, which is what will happen if the feydayeen are not destroyed.

We fought a war for our survival, on this very ground, for many years. We know the languages, the cultures, and the people extraordinarily well. We know the mountain passes and the city streets, the alleys and the highland paths. We have bled with you. And we have Kurdish peshmerga on the ground, as we speak, in small numbers in Mosul. Pitifully small numbers, in my estimation. If I was an American political commander in the region, I would not hesitate to enlist the Kurds. And fight an all-out counter-guerrilla war against the feydayeen, al Qaeda, and Al Ansar Islam. Go after the bastards, track them, and kill them. If you do not aggressively attack the feydayeen, they will exploit American indecisiveness and loss of nerve and you will lose Iraq. Which would bring back Ba'athist fascism and provide Osama bin Laden with a huge base to launch terror attacks against Israel, Iraqi Kurdistan, Kuwait, Europe, and America. Please tell the Americans that we lost 300 Kurds up north, here in northern Iraq, to help defeat Saddam. And we would lose 3,000 more if it meant defeating and destroying the feydayeen. We will stand and fight with Americans to keep Iraq free, at a moment's notice. Let the Kurdish peshmerga, both PUK and KDP, patrol and hunt down and kill the feydayeen. Form joint patrols, of American paratroopers and Kurdish peshmerga. And you will see an end to feydayeen in Mosul, in a week, and an end to the feydayeen in the Sunni triangle, in a month. We can speak Arabic and we have been fighting and surviving, against impossible odds, for a very long time here. Our fighters and our commanders are brave, blooded, and clever. And I say this, finally, to any American or anyone else who thinks Saddam should have remained in power: Live one day under Saddam's dictatorship and tell me you enjoyed it. I have lived all my life under his fascism and my people have seen horrors only the Jews, otherwise, have seen. Like the Jews, we have seen hell on earth. And hell is over, thanks to America. Hell is over!

My people can walk Kurdish streets in peace and freedom and dignity and there are many of us who thought we would never, never see days like these, days when we could speak of Saddam's dictatorship in the past tense. My children and my wife can sleep every night now, knowing that Ba'athist fascists are never coming back to power. Knowing that Saddam is finished, forever. We can sleep without fear now, every night.

Before April 9, 2003, we always felt the shadow of fear from Baghdad. But no more. We have already taken positive steps to ensure that our new-found freedom endures. The new mayor of Kirkuk is Kurdish. He is the gentleman that the Turkish commandos were conspiring to assassinate in early July. It is getting on to mid-August, and he remains in power. Also, the governor of Kirkuk province is Kurdish. Kirkuk will stay in Iraqi Kurdistan, and it will be the capital of Iraqi Kurdistan. It is a great irony, for Saddam tried to steal Kirkuk from the Kurds for thirty-five years.

My father was born in Kirkuk, and my grandfather had much property in Kirkuk. My grandfather died in 1963, and under Iraqi law, we could only sell the land to an Iraqi Arab, not to a Kurd. Nor could we build a house on the property we owned, because only Arabs were allowed to do that. Saddam was evil in many ways, you see. But Saddam's time is gone. Hell is over. We have prevailed! We can control the oil in Kirkuk. Kurds can control the oil! We will use this money for schools and hospitals, not to kill babies with chemical bombs and to pay Mukhabarat secret police to rape and torture and murder. And not to pay Palestinian suicide bombers, as Saddam did. What a butcher Saddam was. Saddam always invested in death, not life. Now, he will discover how wrong his investments were, how deeply wrong he was.

For my people, I wish the same as for my family: to be free. I hope and dream that all Kurds have a good life, with happiness, and not to be thinking only about money. To have peace in the heart and freedom from fascism. And I want Kurdistan to be an independent state, eventually. And we will never live under a dictatorship, again. Never again, Saddam! *Kurdi zin duah, Kurdi zin duah!*

With all humanity, we seek to live in peace and security. I have many relatives in America who have already returned to liberated Iraq. I hope many Kurds return, to build the new democratic Iraq. And I must tell you something, something I want all Americans to know. Whenever I see an American soldier, if I am walking in Hawlerr or Dahuk, I shake his hand, and tell him how grateful I am that he came so far to liberate us from the damnation of Saddam's dictatorship. Thanks to the Americans, I can take my children to the Dahuk Art Gallery now, with my beloved wife, and walk without fear and never lie to my children again. I can tell them they have a beautiful future and I feel so good inside, to tell them this truth. And I know, now, that my Kurdish brothers and sisters can paint and sculpt and create with freedom, with freedom from the dictatorship, forever. My good friend and brother-in-law, Seerwan Shakkurr, no longer has to smuggle his magnificent paintings across the Turkish border in the cold and snow, wondering if he will be caught and imprisoned, imprisoned for the crime of being an artist who seeks to live free and shatter the shackles and chains of the dictatorship. Ah, the chains and shackles have been removed, thank God. What price can you set on freedom? Freedom is a priceless gift, a treasure beyond all treasures. A wealth that keeps paying you back, freedom, yes, it is endless wealth, all in itself. Freedom is priceless. Freedom creates all opportunities for a good life, but without freedom life is nothing, nothing but brutal drudgery. Yes, man, freedom is precious. Hell is over. And we have America to thank for that.

RELIGIOUS TOLERANCE AND COMPASSION

Ablahhad Afram Sawa

President, Chaldean Democratic Union Party
Interviewed: August 25, 2003

> "Religion should be about love, justice and
> compassion, not murder."

Ablahhad Afram, President of the Chaldean Union Democratic Party, is well-versed with the history of Iraq. He mentions with pride that Chaldeans ruled Iraq 3,000 years ago, in the days when Babylon was the capital of Mesopotamia. The most renowned Chaldean king in history was Nabu-Kid-Nasir, whose reign is considered the Golden Age of the Chaldean Kingdom (605 B.C.–562 B.C.). He built the Hanging Gardens of Babylon, one of the Seven Wonders of the World, to please his wife, Queen Ameets, who missed the mountain greenery of her youth in the Zagros Mountains, the spectacular highlands which spread throughout Iraqi Kurdistan and western Iran. The Chaldean Kingdom spread from the Mediterranean to the Persian Gulf, and north to the great Lake Wan in Iran. During King Nabu-Kid-Nasir's era, Babylon entered its time of glory, with decades of scientific, agricultural, and artistic achievement unparalleled in Mesopotamian history.

Today, the Chaldean Catholics and Assyrians, whose Catholic services resemble those of the Chaldeans—very short Mass that's never more than twenty minutes, while women sit on one side of the church, men on the other—number around 30,000 in Kurdistan, northern Iraq. I had traveled to the ancient Christian village of Al Quosh to meet with the President. We sat in a courtyard as a lean, hard-looking bodyguard scanned the barren rocky ridgelines. It was dusk in Iraqi Kurdistan and young shepherds drifted back with flocks of sheep from the rolling golden fields that command the southern and eastern approaches to the mountain town. Ablahhad laughed and told us that he never dreamed, in his youth as a shepherd, that he'd lead his Chaldean people as a politician. His bodyguard grinned and said, in Chaldean, "Life is a mysterious thing, Mr. President."

The Chaldean leader has known Al Quosh all his life. Only now, he said, does he feel Al Quosh and all Chaldean Catholics have a future. He was born in a small Chaldean farming village deep in the mountains, some fifty kilometers north of Al Quosh, in 1951. The name of his village was Maria-Yako, meaning the village of Mary and Jacob, the mother of Jesus and grandson of Abraham. The Iraqi Army, under Saddam Hussein's Ba'athist dictatorship, bombed and destroyed Maria-Yako in 1988. He rubbed his deeply-wrinkled forehead and said there is talk of rebuilding Maria-Yako. The stones lie scattered, he said, and the gathered leadership of his political party which represented Chaldean Catholics throughout Iraq, the Chaldean Democratic Union Party, approved reconstructing Maria-Yako. One of the churches in Al Quosh, a massive stone temple, dates back 1,800 years; the building survived Saddam.

■　■　■

It would be good to rebuild the village with its ancient stones that gave shelter to many centuries of Chaldean families. For the stones hold the spirits of the ancients, and we'd honor their spirits by rebuilding the village. It would not be easy. But God gives us courage to live our dreams.

We lived high in the mountains in Maria-Yako, when I was a young man. The village was beautiful. There were French Dominican nuns and priests there, teaching us in Catholic schools. They were kind to come so far to teach us, and they helped us so much. For instance, Maria-Yako was the first village in all of Iraq to plant tomatoes, in 1903. The nuns and priests brought the seeds from France. Prior to that time, people here had no idea what tomatoes were—at first, people were afraid to eat the tomatoes!

In my youth, I helped my family with our farm and our livestock. Even as a small boy, I was a shepherd, and tended to my family's flocks of sheep. My primary school was at the Christian village of Shezee. Like Maria-Yako, Shezee was bombed and destroyed by Saddam's dictatorship, during the hellish Al Anfal chemical attacks and reign of terror in 1987 and 1988. And it's not impossible, to rebuild Maria-Yako. As it says in Mark 10:27, "For with God, all things are possible." The great challenge is first, building a road up to the village. To make a road there, where the mountain has such steep and twisting ways, is necessary if the village itself is going to be rebuilt. It would be a great testament to the liberation of Iraq, to show that we prevailed, thank God and America, after so many years of Saddam's terror.

The Ba'athists segregated us Christians, all Chaldean Catholics, from our Kurdish brothers and sisters. This was Saddam's fascism, of course. It was in that time, in the early 1970s, that Saddam Hussein started shading Islamic rules with Ba'athist rules—these rules oppressed Christians and also, pitted Sunni against Shia. For instance, one of Saddam's laws, which appealed strongly to radical fundamentalist Islamists and brought in great amounts of money from Wahabi Muslims in Saudi Arabia, was the rule that if either the father or mother converts to Islam, the children automatically become Islamic. For example, say there is an Iraqi Christian family of six, the children are grown, perhaps even married themselves. If either the father or mother, in the original family of six, converts to Islam, then all four children automatically become Muslim and thus, so do their children. Saddam offered money to people to do this, religious bribes, so to speak. The money came from the Wahabi Muslim clerics in Saudi Arabia.

Death is the penalty for conversion from Islam to another faith, by the way. Death in Iraq, and in all the Middle East. This is the thing about Islam that has always confounded me. Religion should be about love, justice and compassion, not murder. The Buddhists, Hindu, and Christians, in my view, have a deeper understanding of human nature, on this issue. Faith is a matter of the heart and no one has the right to punish you for choosing to follow a path different from their own. There is one story from the Bible, that captures the essence of Christianity. The story of Jesus Christ forgiving the woman of adultery. This is the essence of Christianity, forgiveness. Love is many things, and Christ's love bears forgiveness deep within it. And remember, Christ said to the woman, "Go, and sin no more." He saved her life, of course, but he also left her with words to ponder on how to live a good life. I think this is a beautiful story, because Jesus is saying to the world, all of us are sinners; none of us can judge this woman. "'Let he who is without sin cast the first stone,'" said Jesus. The other part of this story that is very telling is that the women of that time, in the Middle East, were so oppressed. If the men made sins, there was little or no punishment. Yet women were stoned, brutally killed, for adultery, a sin which men scoffed at. This was a terrible blow against women. The fight for women's rights, carried out today by women such as Jula Hajee [Editor's Note: See page 117.] begins with the battle against such injustice, long ago. I love this story, also, because Jesus paused in the middle of this life-or-death situation and reflected on it, before saving the woman's life with his words. You see, Jesus knew the importance of patience, even in the heat of the moment. And he did not hesitate, once he knew he had to do the right thing. Christ was a man of love, justice and peace. Justice without love is incomplete, and real peace, without love, is impossible. Peace without justice is tyranny.

In Baghdad, and much of Iraq, if you were not a member of the Ba'athist party, it was very difficult to get employed. And as a Christian, there was great bias against me, as against all Christians under Saddam's dictatorship. In 1977, for instance, when I was twenty-six, Saddam put enormous pressure on Chaldeans to change our Iraqi identification cards from Chaldean to Arab. If you wanted to buy a piece of land or a house, you first had to change your ID card to Arab. This was part of Saddam's Arabization program, which caused great suffering to the Kurds and Chaldeans in northern Iraq. And the Soriya massacre was not the only war crime Saddam's Ba'athists perptrated against us. Saddam ordered ninety-one Chaldean Catholic families held at a fort near the Turkish border, in 1988. These families were taken, blindfolded—their hands bound behind them—and buried alive in trenches at Al Nasiriyah. I believe your Marines fought valiantly at Al Nasiriyah, in March and April of this year.

Saddam destroyed many Christian churches, also. Between the fall of 1987 and the creation of the safe haven in northern Iraq, in 1991, Saddam destroyed nearly every church in the Chaldean villages of Iraqi Kurdistan. Some of these churches were well over 1,000 years old. And he was brutal in other ways to Christians, also. Saddam re-possessed all Catholic private schools and gave them to his Ba'athist government. These schools were connected, on the same property, to the Catholic churches they belonged to. So, by doing this, Saddam also repossessed the churches, and the property on which they stood. Our Chaldean Catholics in these villages and towns began praying in nearby caves, in makeshift temples in the mountains, and in their homes—they no longer had churches to gather in. And after the Gulf War in 1991, Saddam wanted to appeal to Muslim extremists. Saddam made a law to close all the bars—60,000 bars throughout Iraq—and forbid any Muslim from owning a bar. Saddam knew, of course, that Christians owned all the bars in Iraq. So, many families starved as a result of this law. And they were all Christian families.

You know, an American reporter asked me before the war to liberate Iraq, "Aren't you afraid that President George W. Bush will order an attack on Iraq?" I laughed and he asked why I was laughing, for war is a serious thing. And I mentioned to him that indeed, war is a serious thing and so is justice, and that is why I am laughing, for it was clear he had no understanding of the horror Saddam had so long perpetrated against us. And I told him, "We are afraid of only one thing, truly. We are afraid that America will not attack. For if America does not attack, Saddam will remain in power. And we despise living under his dictatorship, even in the so-called safe haven of northern Iraq."

You know, it was your great American writer Hemingway who once said, "There are worse things than war and they all come with defeat." Hemingway spoke truth, when he said that. Many times, over the years, I have read *For Whom the Bell Tolls*, and gained strength and courage from it. The story is timeless. I have seen worse things than war, all my life. The injustices and brutality Saddam perpetrated against the Kurds, against my people, against all Iraqis who desired liberty, these are far worse than war and worth fighting against, worth fighting a war to destroy and eradicate, forever. Rape and torture and murder all come with defeat—what the Kurds endured, my God, you can see why our Kurdish brothers and sisters were so eager to fight and destroy Saddam's dictatorship. And they all come with defeat, if you are on the losing end and a dictatorship gains the upper hand. So yes. Hemingway clearly understood this. There is nothing sweeter than destroying a dictatorship, if you have lived under one—to see these days with my own eyes, days of victory and joy, brings me great happiness and contentment. The war to liberate Iraq was noble and just, without question.

There is great hope, now, for Iraq's road to freedom. My hope is that minorities, such as Chaldean Catholics and Assyrian Christians, live in a democratic Iraq and retain our human rights. We must live in a way that promotes democracy, tolerance, and freedom. Our neighboring countries in northern Iraq—Syria, Turkey, and Iran—have governments which detest democracy. But we will not be denied! We have our chance now, an opportunity we long have dreamed would come true! And should the Kurds seek independence, we Chaldeans will not oppose a free independent nation of Kurdistan.

We are not without difficult days—I, myself, protested to Paul Bremer in July 2003 about the lack of Chaldean representation on the interim ruling council, but that issue can be resolved, once we hold our own elections. This is a time of great political activity for me, and for all Iraqis. Just having the freedom to travel and to speak freely, to express differing views, is a luxury.

THE TURNING POINT

Masrour Barzani

Member of the KDP Politboro
Interviewed: July 26, 2003

> "Remember, we have been living in a very
> tough neighborhood for a long time. And we
> have survived, and prevailed."

In the mid-afternoon of July 26th, four days after the brilliant Coalition Special Operations raid on Uday and Qusay Hussein's hideout in Mosul, I was fortunate to interview Masrour Barzani, member of the KDP Politboro, at the KDP Headquarters Compound, in the Presidential Palace in Salahaddin. Widely recognized as one of the young lions of the Kurdish leadership who will likely play a vital role in the new Iraq, Barzani is well-known for being both forthright and eloquent. He had returned to Iraqi Kurdistan in February 2003 to aid the Kurds in the Iraqi War. He speaks English with a sharp, distinct American accent.

He's a stocky, strong, amiable man with a great shock of dark hair and serious, hard-set eyes. Physically, he has the hawk nose of his father, KDP president Massoud Barzani, and his grandfather, the legendary Mala Mustafa Barzani. He wore a midnight blue double-breasted suit, a blue shirt, gold tie, and a warm smile. He shook hands firmly and nodded to a large black leather couch opposite his own. He had two bodyguards. One carried an AK-47 and stood near me, just behind me to my left. The other carried a sidearm in a shoulder holster and stood in the doorway leading to a stone-floored, high-ceilinged foyer where sunlight flooded from a skylight.

■　■　■

My thanks to General Babakher for talking with you of the health of my uncle, General Wajee. He was nearly killed near Hawlerr by friendly fire. There were Iraqi forces near my uncle. The American pilot was unable to distinguish peshmerga fighters from the Iraqi Army. The pilot could not distinguish between the peshmerga and the Iraqis. The damned sad thing is we were minutes from taking the field. But this is war. It was a wild situation. There were many peshmerga, closing in with RPG-7s and small arms, closing in on other Iraqi tanks from two sides. We had captured one Iraqi tank and it was held by us, at one key intersection.

Peshmerga commanded high ground all around. The U.S. Army 10th Group Special Forces were fighting with us, and fighting very hard. Special Forces warriors were coordinating air strikes on the Iraqis, and shooting and moving, helping direct the combat, fighting very skillfully. The Iraqi tanks were clustered around another key road intersection. In the heat and confusion of battle, the American pilot mistook our peshmerga and U.S. Special Forces, at the key intersection where we held one Iraqi tank, for the Iraqi Army.

Strangely, I'd warned my uncle the night before to take especially good care, in the battle to come; we all anticipated heavy fighting. It is a miracle at all that my uncle is alive. The first field surgeon to see him in Hawlerr, a U.S. Army surgeon, said that he'd be dead within thirty-two hours. But he helped my uncle extraordinarily, and eventually, he was stabilized at a hospital in Germany, before being flown on to America. He is better, but still paralyzed. It was very unfortunate but we, my family and all Kurds, accept this in the course of war. Wajee is my father's brother, and we have lost many of our family in the long struggle for Kurdish dignity and freedom.

Thirty-seven people in my family were executed by Saddam. Their only crime was that they were Kurdish and Barzani. They were buried in a mass grave near the Saudi border in 1983. Saddam thought no one would ever find the unmarked mass grave of murdered Barzanis. Just as Saddam never envisioned all the recent mass graves being revealed to all mankind as testament to his genocide against the Kurds. Two hundred thousand Kurds were murdered by Saddam and his army and secret police, the Mukhabarat. Their only crime was that they were Kurdish.

General Babakher and Muhammad Mala Khader spoke truth, you know, about the "many, many Halapjas" in Kurdish highlands. Only 500 villages, roughly, survived Saddam's Al Anfal. Halapja was but one of many barbaric uses of chemical weapons against Kurdish villages. In the mountains and valleys you've seen, and will see, we once had 5,000 Kurdish villages, prior to 1983. Since 1983, Saddam executed a genocidal assault on Kurds. He destroyed 4,500 villages—many were never rebuilt. He herded the Kurds into concentration camps, behind barbed wire. Our mountains, and many of our road-side areas, near our remaining villages, are poisoned with landmines. With a concerted, intense international effort, it will take at least twenty years to remove all of Saddam's mines

In our mountain villages, electricity, hospitals, and schools are the primary needs. Of course, overall security for Kurdistan is crucial. But getting electricity to our remote villages, building hospitals and clinics, and establishing schools in our remote mountain villages is very important, very needful for the poorest Kurds.

There is deep, solid cooperation between all of the Kurdish leadership and the American political leadership, at all levels. All indications are that the Americans are equally satisfied. We have discovered many plots, and uncovered many Iraqi Ba'athist agents, over the last few months. We have identified and ended many Iraqi plans to foment terror in Iraq. We could take a greater role in eradicating the Iraqi resistance. We might be better-suited to this task. Indeed, I believe we are very well-suited for this task. Our human intelligence is outstanding. Almost all Kurds, for instance, can speak Arabic fluently.

And we know the many, varied tribes in Iraq all too well. Remember, we have been living in a very tough neighborhood for a long time. And we have survived, and prevailed.

We've offered our full support to the interim ruling council of Iraq, on which Massoud Barzani, Jalal Talabani, and Hosheyar Zebari sit. And of course, we offer our full and complete support to America and the Coalition. Our goals are the same: eradication of Ba'athist loyalists and all feydayeen. Iraq will be free, democratic and federal.

Saddam's sons, Uday and Qusay, were killed in an area which is reflective of the challenge in Mosul: Mosul has always had a high percentage of the Ba'athist fascist elite. Saddam kept his Mosul palace very well taken care of, for this same reason, to protect the Ba'athist elite. To a great degree, this is the problem with the feydayeen in all Iraq. The Ba'athists are protecting them. Mosul, of course, fell without heavy fighting. But we did not eradicate the Iraqi Army, they melted back, disappeared their uniforms but not their weapons, and faded into the Iraqi Arab neighborhoods of Mosul. Now, the Ba'athist loyalists in Mosul, who enjoyed Saddam's dictatorship and detest freedom for all Iraqis, are continuing to re-organize resistance cells. They are well-funded and very well-trained. Sunni privilege, moreover, and intricate tribal links make it difficult to break up their underground. Difficult, but by all means, not impossible.

I hope to see an independent Kurdistan, and that is my personal dream too. I hope all Kurds can be whatever they choose, to have the freedom to achieve their dreams and to live in dignity, with justice and peace. If federalism in Iraq is the best we can have, so be it. In my heart, I would like to see a free and independent Kurdistan. But reality says, this is far too difficult, now. You know, when you look at European history, the dreams of individuals for national sovereignty often took long and very bloody paths to achieve. We Kurds have seen very difficult times. We have been under siege, from all directions, for nearly a century. We want to leave bloody history behind. And we have an opportunity, now, to be patient, work together with all Iraqis for a democratic federal Iraq, and achieve federalism in Kurdistan.

We never had the chance to represent ourselves in the past. We were never able to give a Kurdish face to the Kurdish struggle. The Turks spoke to the world about us. The Syrians spoke to the world about us. The Arabs and Iranians spoke to the world about us, but we never spoke to the world about us. Our Kurdish voices were silenced and ignored.

Always, before, other people undermined the dignity, honor, history and reality of Kurds. Now is a crucial time for us. We are able to speak freely and without fear! The liberation of Iraq from Ba'athism is a fundamental turning point for the Kurds. This is a sea-change time in Kurdish history. We can speak for ourselves and the world is finally listening. We can unite our people and help restore dignity to all Iraq, and we are praised. And this is due, in no small part, to the process that began in 1991, with the safe haven. When the people of other countries, influenced by global communications and human rights reports, pressured home demands for a safe haven and no-fly zone, we knew we would overcome.

But the main thing now is the support coming from the American people, and all people who cherish freedom. We greatly appreciate the aid we've received. And our close ties with the Coalition must continue, but the most important thing is the intense, spirited support of Americans, the grass roots. Once that bond is reinforced, set in concrete, democracy and freedom in Kurdistan will stand for all eternity.

EPILOGUE:
Listen to the Kurds

Back in the Kurdish highlands after returning from Fallujah on Valentine's Day, 2004, I was told by a source in Coalition intelligence that cleric Muqtada Al Sadr, leader of 10,000 Shia militia fighters in southern Iraq, has strong ties to Imad Fayez Mugniyah, Hizbollah's top security chief and plotter of suicide bombing attacks. Mugniyah, second on the Federal Bureau of Investigation's Most Wanted Terrorist list, was behind many attacks on Americans, including the 1983 Beirut bombing of U.S. Marines and the 1983 bombing of the U.S. Embassy in Beirut.

By means of car bombs and suicide attacks, Shia brigands, al Qaeda terrorists, and Ba'athist generals—not the Coalition or the nascent Iraqi government—control the iniative in the Iraqi War. Al Sadr, who remains wanted on a conspiracy-to-murder warrant, continues to spread terror in Iraq. Al Qaeda–linked Jordanian Abu Massab al-Zarqawi, who was behind the beheading of American Nicholas Berg, roams at will throughout Iraq, terrorizing anyone whom he declares is not a friend of radical Islam. When power was turned over to the interim Iraqi government on June 28, 2004, Coalition efforts in effect became the war that President Bush had failed to win. This vast and lethal campaign may, in time, be remembered as the war that removed Saddam Hussein but emboldened Ba'athists throughout Iraq.

General Babakher Zebari and other prominent Kurds warned Major General David L. Petraeus in May and June, 2003, that the American failure to strike and kill Ba'athists, to disarm Iraqis, and to crush the Iraqi Army would not go unnoticed by the Iraqi insurgency and radical Islamic terrorists. But we failed to listen to the Kurds, whose intelligence is gained from human sources and facts on the ground: they watch, look, listen, and learn. They know the languages, know the terrain, know the markets, know the temples, and know the people.

Fifty-nine years ago, in Vietnam, Americans disregarded ground intelligence and paid the price. In autumn 1945, a team from the CIA's precursor, the Office of Strategic Services, was rebuffed and ignored both in Vietnam and upon its return to Washington, D.C.

Throughout the summer of 1945 the team, led by Army Major Archimedes L. A. Patti, fought alongside Ho Chi Minh and his Viet Minh guerrilla fighters, attacking and cutting Japanese supply lines running from southern China into northern Vietnam, and also rescued downed Allied pilots.

Major Patti earned his combat wisdom on raids and patrols with Viet Minh in the highlands and paddies of northern Vietnam in the summer of 1945. Major Patti came back from Vietnam with one clear understanding—clear to him, but not to people in Washington who had spent zero time in the field in Vietnam: Ho Chi Minh was the revered leader of the Vietnamese people, especially the peasantry. That remains true today and is eternal in Vietnam.

In 1945 in Vietnam, the peasants were the power. Vietnamese farmers were the backbone of the Viet Minh's popular support and they wanted the Viet Minh to rule an independent Vietnam. That desire never changed. Major Patti understood that clearly, he saw it—he'd lived that truth.

He'd walked the ridgelines and cut bamboo and eaten rice cooked over wood fires and smelled the fragrant scent of bougainevillea and water buffalo manure. He knew the rice paddies and the mountain passes. He'd listened to the guerrilla fighters, and to farmers and their families in Vietnam.

Major Patti returned to Washington with letters from Ho Chi Minh to President Harry S. Truman. These letters, which were delivered to the Department of State's Far Eastern desk, urged U.S. recognition of the independent Republic of Vietnam. But Truman never saw the letters, and a potential ally in Southeast Asia was set adrift.

There is a monument in Washington, directly across from the State Department at 22nd and Constitution Avenue, NW. On the monument are 58,000 reasons why we must not lose the war in Iraq: names of all those killed in action in Vietnam, engraved on a wall of black granite.

In autumn 1945, the American government denied itself key ground intelligence in Southeast Asia, as it is denying itself key intelligence from the field in Southwest Asia in 2004. The Kurds today remain ignored, their counsel unheeded, and their vast combat wisdom a saber that the Coalition never unsheathed.

There remains no permanent security agreement with the Kurds—allies who have not, it should be pointed out, attacked, killed, beheaded, or kidnapped Americans and Coalition forces. The Kurds bled with us to free Iraq. Our thanks for their sacrifice and their undying loyalty was to disarm them, as Major General Petreaus ordered in Mosul in 2003. We also disregarded their human intelligence, and ignoring information from people far better-versed in the culture, languages, and terrain than yourself has historically been a recipe for failure.

Why has President George W. Bush failed to win the Iraq War? For his entire life he has been surrounded by business and politics. He has never seen action. He has no first-hand experience in combat and his personality is not one suited for war. President Bush's refusal to reward and to listen to the Kurds has denied American warriors in Iraq vital ground intelligence that could have ended this war in 2003.

■ ■ ■

The Kurds have the best ground intelligence in Iraq because they have sources everywhere. Moreover, they communicate very well—open lines of communication reach from all sectors of Kurdish society to Kurdish peshmerga and Kurdish intelligence. Recently, a sixty-five-year-old man arrived on my base with information about an Al-Zarquawi cell that had just entered Dahuk. After he informed Kurdish intelligence officers, he was thanked and went home. He was not paid—Kurds see it as their sworn duty to fight terrorism, regardless of their station or position.

U.S. Army military intelligence and Kurdish military intelligence were responsible for the only captures of al Qaeda terrorists I've witnessed in Iraq. Other than sources it paid, the CIA has no human intelligence network inside the heart of Iraq. And these paid sources had been developed over the thirty-five years Saddam Hussein ruled Iraq with an iron fist and chemical weapons.

We need a commander-in-chief who understands the complexities of war, especially guerrilla war, and who also understands the need to be engaged, clever, unwavering, and relentless in fighting the war.

Not listening kills you in love and war. President Bush, and many of his generals, refused to listen to the Kurds and still do. This indifference, along with Bush's success at ensuring that former Ba'athist generals and sheikhs are well taken care of in post-Saddam Iraq, has emboldened the Iraqi insurgency. The U.S. has embittered and angered the only people in Iraq who are combat-proven allies, and paved a road for a Ba'athist revival. Only fifteen months ago, on May 1, 2003, from the deck of an aircraft carrier off San Diego, President Bush declared that "All major combat has ended in Iraq." Three days earlier, in Fallujah, on April 28, 2003, the Coalition had retreated in the face of a riot; roughly a year later in the same city, First Marines slugged it out in close-quarter combat with Saddam loyalist feydayeen and al Qaeda for much of April. And again, the Coalition retreated. The Marines have now lost Fallujah, enabling anti-coalition forces there to re-arm, regroup, and re-deploy.

Losing key terrain is how nations lose wars. Fallujah, situated on major feydayeen supply routes running to the two primary feydayeen sanctuaries—Syria and Iran—is decidedly key terrain. Fallujah, as I write, remains uncaptured.

The Kurdish intelligence network includes Fallujah. But, as General Babakher Zebari told me in late July 2003, "The Americans refuse to listen to us and they deny critical intelligence; the Americans fear the Turks and the Arabs that much. You can't win a war if you don't listen to people who were fighting your enemy here before your present generals marched as cadets on parade at West Point. You've lost key terrain because of the U.S. refusal to heed Kurdish counsel."

10th Group Special Forces commandos—who worked in early 2003 with General Zebari to plan actions before the start of the war in Northern Iraq—told me in March 2004 that Zebari was so frustrated and angered by the Coalition's stonewalling of the Kurds that he refused to meet with them when they returned to northern Iraq in January 2004. These commandos reported that it took a series of phone calls and apologies over ten days just for 10th Group to sit down with him. The trust these men had built with Zebari had broken down that badly that it is only now being rebuilt.

General Zebari's earlier assertions were not lost on some U.S. Army infantry lieutenants. First Lieutenant Adam Bohlen of Titusville, Florida, with the Tenth Mountain Division, is a Fallujah veteran. Much of the key terrain in Iraq—Baghdad, Mosul, the Ba'athist strongholds of Fallujah, Tikrit, Ramadi, and Baquoubah—was, in the words of Lieutenant Bohlen, ". . . seized but not secured, held but not held down. You have to fully commit to win a war, you have to clear streets and houses, kill the enemy, destroy your enemy's will to fight, deny him all key terrain, and eliminate all his weapons and supplies. Look at Fallujah. It was never cleared and secured—we had the magnificent opportunity to crush and kill the Iraqi Army, destroy their weapons, and secure all key terrain, in April and May 2003."

War never changes. If you want to win a war, you must crush and kill the enemy. You must destroy your enemy's will to fight. You must clear, hold, and secure key terrain. That is true in every war, be it guerrilla warfare or conventional combat.

The Bush administration's refusal to heed Kurdish counsel haunts America and the Coalition in the Iraqi War. The Coalition has lost Fallujah, Mosul has a deeply entrenched insurgency, and neither of those facts has altered President Bush's actions as commander-in-chief: He continues to overlook the Kurds.

As the Kurds told us in spring 2003, we had the opportunity to drive a stake through the heart of Ba'athism. That opportunity has now been lost forever. The consequences of President Bush's indecisive leadership have been tragic for Coalition warriors, and deeply troubling for the future of Iraq.

Kurdish women activists from Dahuk and Zakho, for instance, have stopped traveling to Mosul and no longer hold meetings there, for fear of being murdered by feydayeen or al Qaeda. As a consequence, many Kurdish women in Mosul no longer have opportunities to organize unions, pool resources for jointly owned small businesses, and forge a brighter future for their children in post-Saddam Iraq. As the prominent Kurdish activist Jula Hajee said on July 3, 2004, in Dahuk, "What have the Americans done in Mosul, other than support Ba'athists? Mosul is not safe to travel in, or meet in. The Ba'athists are just as strong in Mosul now as they were under Saddam."

When Major General Petraeus appointed one of Saddam's generals, the prominent Ba'athist Ghanim Al Basso, as governor of Ninevah and mayor of Mosul, in May 2003, he rewarded all

Ba'athists in Iraq, and he punished all Kurds who had fought to free this country from Ba'athism. The Kurdish leadership, according to Masrour Barzani, repeatedly told U.S. military leadership and civilian leadership in Iraq that their appointment of Al Basso would spell disaster for the Coalition, embolden the then-building Iraqi insurgency, and deny the Coalition the best intelligence and best guerrilla fighters in Iraq.

■   ■   ■

A Coalition Special Operations commando told me on May 7, 2004, in Dahuk, "If I give you my name, rank and unit, I can kiss my career in Special Ops goodbye. But I will tell you this: Petraeus burned a lot of bridges to the Kurds here and he built bridges to Ba'athists, left and right, without once stopping and thinking about the consequences of his actions. He handed out money to Arab contractors up north with Ba'athist ties, before wells were even dug on those contracts. The Ba'athist-connected contractors got paid and the villagers are asking 'where's our water?' Petraeus denied key intelligence on feydayeen, simply because it came from the Kurds. And Ghanim Al Basso, as we now know, was actively funding, aiding, and supporting feydayeen, through his feydayeen commander brother, in Mosul and northern Iraq. Ghanim Al Basso was Petraeus' gift to the Iraqi insurgency. Thanks to Petraeus, the insurgency up north is stronger, deeper, and very well-financed; Petraeus had the chance to annihilate the feydayeen and really strike hard at al Qaeda up here and he pissed it away. In war, there are no second chances."

Ba'athist war criminal Abdul Kharim Jahayshee, who led the Soriya Massacre in Iraqi Kurdistan on August 16, 1969, is walking free in Mosul; Fallujah is controlled by Saddam's generals, just as it was during Saddam's Ba'athist dictatorship; al Qaeda is free to build its cells in Fallujah; and Mosul now has the deepest-layered and best-organized feydayeen cell network in Iraq, according to sources in Coalition Special Operations. Some 80 percent of the contracts on U.S. military bases in Fallujah and western Iraq were awarded to notorious Ba'athist and confidante of Saddam Hussein, Sheikh Gazi Al Bowisa.

When Iraqi imams in Mosul preach for Muslims to hail al Qaeda and Al Ansar Islam, and to kill Kurds and Americans and all Coalition forces, they're speaking the language of war, not the language of the Pentagon or the White House or Foggy Bottom or Langley. Yet the Kurds understand what those imams are saying.

What the Kurds understand most of all is that the ancient laws of war are exactly the same today as they were at Cunaxa in 401 B.C., when Xenophon the Athenian seized command in a desperate battle against Persians led by King Artaxerxes, just a gull's flight from present-day Fallujah. They are the same as they were for the Kurds fighting the Ba'athists from 1961–1991, on this turf, in northern Iraq.

There is no honorable answer for our warriors. There is no just answer. President Bush has shown no clarity, unity, or consistency in his war-fighting strategy in Iraq.

The Spartans fought valiantly at Thermoplyac because they knew their commanders would honor their sacrifice if they died in battle. The Greeks at Cunaxa likewise knew that their commanders were committed and unwavering in pursuit of victory.

American forces came to Iraq for justice and, it has been asserted, to bring peace to a long-suffering people. It is unclear whether that goal has been attained. As a Kurdish translator said after a successful raid in Mosul on October 3, 2003, "There will be no peace in Iraq until there is justice for all whose lives were destroyed by Ba'athism."

Mike Tucker
August 2004

ACKNOWLEDGMENTS

Gratitude to all below. God bless you.

In the words of the Hmong hilltribes of Southeast Asia, long life and a good death.

■　■　■

Lieutenant J. Robert Kerrey, U.S. Navy SEALS, (ret.). President, New School, New York City.

U.S. Army 10th Group Special Forces, and Kurdish Peshmerga for their actions to liberate Mosul and all of northern Iraq (March–April 2003).

Mrs. Jula Hajee, Kurdistan Women's Union Dahuk branch president, her administrators, and her staff.

Mr. Muhammad Mala Khader, Peshmerga Commander (ret.), and KDP Dahuk Branch president, Dahuk, Iraqi Kurdistan.

Mr. Masrour Barzani, KDP Politboro, KDP HQ, Salahadin, Iraqi Kurdistan.

Mr. Farhad Barzani, KDP Representative, Washington, D.C.

General Babakher Zebari, Commanding General KDP Northern Military Region, Dahuk, Iraqi Kurdistan.

Mr. Faisal Rostinki Dosky, KDP Military Intelligence Chief. Dahuk, Iraqi Kurdistan.

Lieutenant Colonel Randal Campbell, U.S. Army 101st Airborne Division (Air Assault). KDP Liason Officer, Salahadin, Iraqi Kurdistan.

Sergeant First Class Gilbert Ortiz, U.S. Army 101st Airborne Division (Air Assault). Peshmerga Liason Officer, Dahuk, Iraqi Kurdistan.

The students, artists, professors, and staff of the Dahuk Institute of Fine Arts, Dahuk, Iraqi Kurdistan.

The staff of the Dahuk Gallery of Fine Arts, Dahuk.

Mr. Fawsi Mohammad and the faculty and staff at the Roj Center, Dahuk, Iraqi Kurdistan, northern Iraq.

BIBLIOGRAPHY

Hemingway, Ernest. *For Whom the Bell Tolls.* New York: Charles Scribner's Sons, 1940.

Hemingway, Ernest. *The Old Man and the Sea.* New York: Charles Scribner's Sons, 1952.

Hemingway, Ernest. *The Snows of Kilimanjaro and Other Stories.* New York: Charles Scribner's Sons, 1964.

Lewis, Bernard. *The Assassins.* New York: Basic Books, 2003.

McDowall, David. *A Modern History of the Kurds.* London: I. B. Tauris & Co. Ltd, 2000.

Randall, Jonathan. *After Such Knowledge, What Forgiveness?* New York: 1996.

Wiesel, Elie. *Night.* New York: Hill & Wang, 1960.

Xenophon. *The Persian Expedition.* Translator: Rex Warner. London: Penguin, 1949.

INDEX

ABOUT THE AUTHOR

MIKE TUCKER is a poet, writer, photographer, former Marine infantryman and war correspondent. Originally from Maryland, he has traveled extensively in Spain, the Near East, and the Far East. Mr. Tucker lived with Black Lahu, Hmong, and Karen hilltribes in northern Thailand in the 1990s; all told, he lived and worked in Thailand just over five years. Tucker was twice awarded Honors in Poetry at James Madison University, from which he received his bachelor's degree in history in 1982. He received a master's degree from James Madison in 1999.

In July 2003, he journeyed to Iraq via Turkey, where he investigated Ba'athist war crimes in Kurdistan, and saw action alongside U.S. Army snipers, scouts, light infantry, paratroopers, and Coalition Special Ops commandos in Mosul and Fallujah. He remains in Iraq with US Army Special Forces and Kurdish peshmerga in Northern Iraq. *Among Warriors*, his account of his experiences with U.S. troops in Iraq, will be published by The Lyons Press in 2005.